THE COMPLETE IDIOT'S GUIDE TO

Power Words

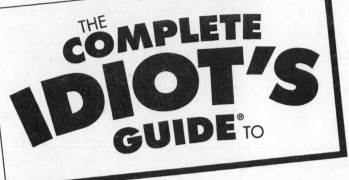

THE COMPLETE IDIOT'S GUIDE® TO

Power Words

by Scott Snair, Ph.D.

ALPHA

A member of Penguin Group (USA) Inc.

To my second mom and dad, Jane and Roy, steadfast sources of love, generosity, and wisdom.

ALPHA BOOKS

Published by the Penguin Group

Penguin Group (USA) Inc., 375 Hudson Street, New York, New York 10014, USA

Penguin Group (Canada), 90 Eglinton Avenue East, Suite 700, Toronto, Ontario M4P 2Y3, Canada (a division of Pearson Penguin Canada Inc.)

Penguin Books Ltd., 80 Strand, London WC2R 0RL, England

Penguin Ireland, 25 St. Stephen's Green, Dublin 2, Ireland (a division of Penguin Books Ltd.)

Penguin Group (Australia), 250 Camberwell Road, Camberwell, Victoria 3124, Australia (a division of Pearson Australia Group Pty. Ltd.)

Penguin Books India Pvt. Ltd., 11 Community Centre, Panchsheel Park, New Delhi   110 017, India

Penguin Group (NZ), 67 Apollo Drive, Rosedale, North Shore, Auckland 1311, New Zealand (a division of Pearson New Zealand Ltd.)

Penguin Books (South Africa) (Pty.) Ltd., 24 Sturdee Avenue, Rosebank, Johannesburg 2196, South Africa

Penguin Books Ltd., Registered Offices: 80 Strand, London WC2R 0RL, England

Copyright © 2009 by Scott Snair, Ph.D.

International Standard Book Number: 978-1-59257-843-6
Library of Congress Catalog Card Number: 2008939793

11   10   09   8   7   6   5   4   3   2   1

Interpretation of the printing code: The rightmost number of the first series of numbers is the year of the book's printing; the rightmost number of the second series of numbers is the number of the book's printing. For example, a printing code of 09-1 shows that the first printing occurred in 2009.

Printed in the United States of America

Note: This publication contains the opinions and ideas of its author. It is intended to provide helpful and informative material on the subject matter covered. It is sold with the understanding that the author and publisher are not engaged in rendering professional services in the book. If the reader requires personal assistance or advice, a competent professional should be consulted.

The author and publisher specifically disclaim any responsibility for any liability, loss, or risk, personal or otherwise, which is incurred as a consequence, directly or indirectly, of the use and application of any of the contents of this book.

Most Alpha books are available at special quantity discounts for bulk purchases for sales promotions, premiums, fund-raising, or educational use. Special books, or book excerpts, can also be created to fit specific needs.

For details, write: Special Markets, Alpha Books, 375 Hudson Street, New York, NY 10014.

Publisher: *Marie Butler-Knight*
Editorial Director: *Mike Sanders*
Senior Managing Editor: *Billy Fields*
Executive Editor: *Randy Ladenheim-Gil*
Development Editor: *Julie Coffin*
Production Editor: *Kayla Dugger*
Copy Editor: *Cate Schwenk*

Cartoonist: *Steve Barr*
Cover Designer: *Bill Thomas*
Book Designer: *Trina Wurst*
Indexer: *Brad Herriman*
Layout: *Ayanna Lacey*
Proofreader: *John Etchison*

Contents at a Glance

Appendixes

Contents

Introduction

You would think, in this high-tech, instant-communication, and instant-gratification world of ours, that getting our point across would be a snap. Not so! In fact, our messages have become diluted. Writing and language skills … well, they aren't what they used to be, and technology, if anything, has hurt the way we relate. Studies suggest that many of us have a tougher time than ever relating to one another with words. The good news is that, if you recognize the situation, adapt to it, and learn those power words and phrases that can push through today's communication clutter, you set yourself apart from others and have a much easier time getting your way.

This book provides forceful (but not pushy) words and phrases that offer punch to an instant message, text message, e-mail, or letter. It also supplies verbal expressions and replies that will help you spear through today's muddle of words and misunderstandings. These words will help you assert yourself and impress and inspire (but not intimidate) others. When necessary, these words will help you change direction.

Admittedly, there's more to effective communication than simply having a healthy vocabulary or the gift of gab. It also involves relatively clear-headed attention between parties, proactive listening techniques, genuine interest, and open-mindedness. But once you've gotten to the point where someone is reading what you've written or listening to what you're saying, hooking someone with a strong word or phrase helps keep that line of communication open and hits your reader/listener with an impact that allows for important and desired follow-up from both sides of the message.

Conversely, many people are afraid to ask for things or don't know the right words to use, so they don't ask. For example, economist Linda Babcock and business researcher Sara Laschever contend that one in five adult women today *never* negotiates over anything! That's a staggering statistic, especially when held up against another Babcock/Laschever finding: when you don't negotiate your first salary, you stand to lose more than half a million dollars over your working years.

Don't kid yourself. Knowing how to use words well gets you things, and not knowing how to use them keeps things out of your reach.

In this world of insecurity, poor social skills, short attention spans, and high-paced, high-volume transmission of irrelevancies, the gift of understanding words and using them well puts you ahead. If you engage in the craft of utilizing power words and phrases, you make yourself more important and more influential. Using words well helps get you what you want.

How to Use This Book

The Complete Idiot's Guide to Power Words is broken down into five parts, each covering a significant way in which dynamic words and phrases can make a difference in your life.

Part 1, "Power Words for Negotiating," examines the words and brief phrases that intensify any type of written message. It looks at those specific ways you can write to convey the meanings you want to get across and to draw the responses that you seek from others.

Part 2, "Power Words for Persuading," considers verbal expressions—as well as their deliveries—that take advantage of how certain words register with people in conversation. It delves into why people respond the way they do to such words and how you can take advantage of these expected reactions.

Part 3, "Power Words as Responses," looks at how today's power-word user responds to other people's statements, questions, and even their anger. It looks at ways you can disarm your verbal opponents and more quickly bring them to your side.

Part 4, "Words and Expressions to Avoid," reviews those words and phrases—many of them commonly used today—that should be avoided and why. When used, these expressions tend to challenge or weaken your credibility, charisma, or appearance of sincerity. This part offers practical alternatives.

Part 5, "Mind Tricks That Aren't (Too) Evil," taps into the secrets of inspiring writers, speakers, and success trainers. It delves into the hidden skills of many of today's most impressive users of power words and what makes these word/mind tricks so clever.

Extras

Aside from the chapter-by-chapter reading, this text contains four special sidebars to guide you through the aesthetics of words and the hidden meanings behind them.

def•i•ni•tion

This sidebar expands on or explains a word that appears in the book. If, for example, you want to ask a rhetorical question, it's helpful to know exactly what a rhetorical question is.

Copy and Paste

This provides advice on a particular power word or phrase that augments the more basic information throughout the chapters. These pointers increase your arsenal of power-word tactics.

Highlight and Delete

This provides suggestions on what types of words and phrases you should avoid in certain—or all—circumstances.

Maximizing Maxim

This sidebar offers useful quotations from successful brandishers of power words.

Acknowledgments

I am deeply grateful to the people who brought me this project and helped me as we carried it out together. At Penguin Alpha: acquisitions editor Michele Wells, executive editor Randy Ladenheim-Gil, development editor Julie Coffin, production editor Kayla Dugger, and copy editor Cate Schwenk. All quintessential *power* editors. At Sheree Bykofsky Associates: Janet Rosen, my highly competent, caring agent, and our wonderful (yet amazingly young) matriarch, Sheree Bykofsky.

I appreciate the generous help and advice from my colleagues at the U.S. Military Academy Preparatory School: John Stibravy, Mike Waller, John Greene, Tom Kelly, Tammy Bongi, Sandra Jang, and Steven Baron. Thanks also to my great bosses at USMA Prep: Tyge Rugenstein and William Krug.

Many thanks to those who have hired me and encouraged me throughout my research in the areas of leadership, higher education, and writing. At Seton Hall University: Philip DiSalvio and Susan Spencer. At Thomas Edison State College: Joseph Santora, Patricia Memminger, Jamie Priester, Ann McKithen, and Susan Fischer. And at the University of Maryland: Alan Sutherland.

A very special thank you to my wife, Mary-Jane Snair, and my daughters, Patti and Katie, for cheering me on and tolerating me as deadlines approached. I love you with all my heart.

Trademarks

Part 1

Power Words for Negotiating

Effective negotiating is not a lost art, but it sure is a changing one. The days of long, deliberative writings are gone, and yet the impact of superior prose is stronger than ever. The challenge is to use strong words and phrases that get your reader's attention, keep it, and ultimately make the impact that you seek. If there's something that needs getting done, your words must clearly and convincingly express the need for a specific action.

Power words and phrases are those that help you control your message and gain maximum advantage from a minimum number of words. Power words "hook" your reader into continuing your letter, e-mail, or instant message. They plainly yet passionately state the points you're making and help seal the deal when it comes to bringing about change. Power words help you make it happen!

Chapter 1

Hook Your Reader

In This Chapter

- ◆ Provoking your reader to read on
- ◆ Offering a magnificent vision of the future
- ◆ Painting issues in extremes and contrasts
- ◆ Writing metaphorically
- ◆ Adding a historical context

Whether you're writing an e-mail message, a handwritten letter, or a commentary for the local paper, you'll have a tough time convincing your readers if you can't get them past the first sentence. The problem these days is that people are flooded with stimuli—much of it designed to garner their attention and sell them stuff. A good *hook* sentence—a clever opening line that catches readers' interest—at the beginning of any written message will help you push through all that stimuli and increase the chance that readers will delve into what you've written.

The hook technique runs contrary to the philosophy that a main topic sentence or thesis sentence should lead an essay. However, it does not contradict the "bottom line up front" tenet, which is covered in Chapter 3. After the hook sentence, you may go directly into your thesis or, after discussing the issue a bit in your first paragraph, end that paragraph with the thesis.

My first book was about how to run a team with fewer and shorter business meetings. Getting it published was proving difficult. One day, I decided to change the hook sentence that began my intro letter to prospective editors and agents. My new hook: "The world is going to hell in a business meeting!" The result? A positive response from 6 out of 36 recipients, a contract with a prominent Manhattan agent, and a contract with the editor of a major publisher. The hook pushed through the dozens of inquiries each of these people had received that day and prompted a few of them to respond with "Send me more information!"

Exaggerate to Get Things Started

Weak: "With a few simple steps, we can improve our situation."

Powerful: "A wonderful future is just around the corner. Here's how we can get there."

> ### Maximizing Maxim _____
>
> In their book *The Complete Idiot's Guide to Getting Published, Fourth Edition*, Sheree Bykofsky and Jennifer Basye Sander say the best attention-getting letters have a strong hook within the first two lines. One of their favorite letters begins with the odd sentence, "Mmmm, chocolate!"
>
> "What's a strong hook?" Bykofsky and Sander ask. "Something that grabs the readers' attention and keeps them reading!"

It doesn't pay to exaggerate the facts, warnings, or benefits of what you're suggesting. But it *does* pay to ham up your introduction a bit. I compare this notion to the "shocked and outraged" phrase I mention a little later in this chapter. This calculated exaggeration throws the reader off, makes her wonder if she did, indeed, read what she just read, and encourages her to continue.

Don't write about small changes. Instead, introduce your reader to an idyllic place, and then tell her how you plan to help her get there.

Remember George McFly in *Back to the Future?* "I am your destiny," he says to his future wife. (Unfortunately, he pronounces it "density" and doesn't show his powerful side until later in the movie.)

Example: "A wonderful future for our city is just around the corner. Here's how we can get there. As mayor, I promise to makes things easier on businesses so more businesses hire and more businesses and jobs move here. I promise to ..."

Suggest a Hypothetical Reality

Weak: "It's a good opportunity, filled with lots of possibilities."

Powerful: "It's as if we discovered a wondrous path to a new world of marvels."

Suppose you were able to catch your reader's attention every time you wrote something. Sound splendid? It should: I just painted a hypothetical picture to get your interest. By inviting someone to imagine a situation more appealing or more fascinating than the one he's currently in, you often spark his curiosity enough to read on.

Example: "It's as if we discovered a wondrous treasure chest full of marvels and now we're simply looking for the key. The key, then, is the donation I'm asking you to make to this new, exciting, lifesaving area of research."

Master Metaphors to Compare Concepts

Weak: "I believe we face an unknown threat."

Powerful: "There's a snake in our midst."

When Ronald Reagan was running for president against Jimmy Carter in 1980, Reagan's campaign ran a television ad talking about a "bear in the woods." The ad, of course, was comparing the Soviet Threat to a bear. What made the ad effective? The comparison was never stated explicitly. That is, instead of saying, "The Soviet Threat is like a bear in the woods" (which still would have been relatively effective), the ad never used the words *like* or *as,* and therefore the bear stood as a *metaphor.* I remember watching that political commercial as a young man and being very taken by it.

def•i•ni•tion

> A **metaphor** is a comparison made without using the words *like* or *as*. It generally packs a more powerful punch than a simile, which is a comparison that does use *like* or *as*.

Rather than penning "the future is as dark as a scary movie," try scrapping *as* and simply write, "the future is a scary movie." The comparison isn't as hammer-over-the-head obvious, but the mild elusiveness of the association makes your reader more likely to read on.

Example: "There's a snake in our midst. And if we allow it to slither around our feet, it's certain to bite and poison us. This snake is the serpent of indifference—the way we walk past a homeless man on the street, or the way we drive past a young woman on the side of the road looking helplessly at a flat tire on her car full of children. Our uncaring ways are the venom that will soon kill us as a people."

Express Your Indignation to the Max

Weak: "Dear Sir or Ma'am, I am writing to complain ..."

Powerful: "Dear Mr. Chief Executive Officer, I am shocked and outraged over my recent treatment ..."

If a company or an organization is doing you wrong, don't write to a customer service person and politely tell how miffed you are. Instead, write to the top dog of the corporation and tell him that you are truly furious and taken aback by how poorly his company has treated you. I have used this sentence to start letters about a miscalculated mortgage payment, a misprocessed federal tax payment, and the mistreatment of a family member by a university professor, among others. In each case, someone high enough in the organization to take action contacted me and addressed my complaint.

Don't abuse this type of letter. But when a company has, without question, treated you wrongly, send the letter to the top and begin it with this power expression.

Example: "Dear Mr. Richpockets, I am shocked and outraged over the treatment I was subjected to by your company last week. When arriving home, I noticed that the $4,000 plasma television I had purchased at one of your stores lodged a family of mice, feasting on the wiring inside. When I attempted to return the TV set, your store manager, Stan Laughsalot, ridiculed me in front of several customers, suggesting that I had placed the mice there, and refused to replace the set ..."

Mention the Surprised Person Who Isn't There

Weak: "People would be surprised if they knew what we were up to."

Powerful: "If the average person were to peek into our lab, he or she would be astonished by our research."

In the study of law, a judge often measures the accused's actions against what a reasonable, informed person in the same situation might do. This "reasonable person" doesn't really exist: it's a model against which to assess actions and reactions.

This fictitious person serves the power writer as well. When you suggest the average person would be blown away by what you're about to tell the reader, you entice her to delve further into your message.

Not to get too hung up on grammar, but it's worth mentioning here that when writing about the surprised, hypothetical person, it's important to use the past subjunctive mood of the verb *be*. Don't write, "If a man was noble, he would be on our side." Instead, use the past subjunctive form *were* and write, "If a man were noble, he would be on our side."

Example: "If the average citizen of this city were to watch these deals happen behind closed doors, he or she would be astonished by and ashamed of how this city council writes its annual budget. This is not your average political give-and-take. It's underhanded cronyism. It's shocking and disgraceful, and it needs to change."

Draw Attention to the Historic Choice

Weak: "We have an important decision to make."

Powerful: "We have reached a historic crossroads."

Sometimes, putting something up front (in terms of black and white) is the best way to garner a reader's interest. This dilemma probably isn't fair: most choices in life involve more than two choices. But as an opener, the display of two extremes is powerful.

When arguing your point, don't unfairly present two choices when, in fact, there are several. You are bound to be called on this false dilemma. However, the tactic of using two extremes is sometimes reasonable as an effective essay or speech opener.

You can get into the supporting details and the other, lesser choices later on in your essay. But as an opener, talk about your selection as a historic fork in the road, each choice leading down a much different, extreme path.

Example: "We have reached a historic crossroads. Do we select the path of mutually assured destruction, or do we take this new path, this new opportunity to foster a working relationship with a long-time adversary?"

Paint a Vision

Weak: "Here are my long-term goals."

Powerful: "Here is a vision for our future."

There's a magnificent future for you—a future where people love what you write and are entranced by your powerful thoughts. A future where people hang on your every word and eagerly wait for whatever you might write or say next. A future where you're in control.

Sound good? Want to read on? Of course you do! You have just been offered a vision that compels any lover of words to want to read on.

A vision is so much better than a goal. Nobody really cares about your goals—even goals that directly benefit him or her. Any way you present them, itemized objectives seem self-focused and full of empty promise.

However, if you write about an idealized mental picture you have for others—a mental picture of a wonderful, prosperous future, for example—well, now you have their attention. If your vision seems the slightest bit attainable, you gain control over others, which is what power words are all about.

Don't be shy. Tell your readers what your ideal solution looks like. Create it in broadstroke, beautiful colors and descriptions. Little kids laughing. Old people singing. Chirping birds draping flowers around people's heads. Make it breathtaking. Stimulate your readers to read on.

> **Maximizing Maxim**
>
> In 1963, Martin Luther King Jr. offered his vision of a better future: "I have a dream that my four little children will one day live in a nation where they will not be judged by the color of their skin but by the content of their character."

Example: "I offer you this vision for our future. I see a nation where health care is a national right instead of a national disgrace—where a simple surgical procedure doesn't bankrupt a person for life."

Make Their Priorities Your Priorities

Weak: "Here are some ways I plan on supporting you."

Powerful: "Your goals are my goals."

Instead of writing to someone about how you're going to support him, why not take your support a step further? Tell the person that if it's important to him, it's important to you. "Your goals are *my* goals. Your aspirations are *my* aspirations."

When you begin a letter with such a phrase, what you're essentially writing is, "Hey, I'm on

> **Copy and Paste**
>
> Take advantage of people's inherent tendency to take care of themselves. When you write for power and influence, keep in mind that people, as they read your words, are subliminally asking themselves, "What's in it for me?"

your side, and I'm going to help you." That's a message everyone wants to read.

Example: "Your goals are my goals. Make no mistake about it. If you hire me, you essentially hire another arm for yourself. From Day One, your priorities are my priorities."

Activate with an Adverb

Weak: "We move on with confidence."

Powerful: "Confidently, we move forward."

There's something about placing an adverb or adverbial phrase at the end of a sentence that just seems, well, weak. Or at least oh so plain.

Do you *really* want to write that the army charged forward with valiance? Yikes—it sounds as if they were a bunch of weenies! However, turn the sentence around a bit. "Valiantly, the army charged forward." Hey, now *that* sounds like one brave army. What changed things so dramatically? Placing the adverb at the front of the sentence.

By leading with the adverb, you take your writing away from the standard subject-verb-adverb format. More important, you emphasize the adverb. "Bravely, we take on all future challenges." "Proudly, we take stock in the past year's achievements." Ideally, I begin a powerful sentence with an adverb. (Hey, I just did!)

Keep in mind, though, that you should not start *every* sentence with an adverb. The best writing has a variety of long, poignant sentences and short, germane ones. A power word or phrase is most effective when it appears within a clever mix of other kinds of words and sentences.

Example: "Confidently, we move forward. We have the talent, the experience, and the solidarity to enter these uncharted waters. Amazing and rewarding discoveries lie ahead."

Refer to Legacy

Weak: "What will people think?"

Powerful: "How will history judge us?"

As psychologist Abraham Maslow argued in the 1940s, belonging to a group holds forceful sway over people's emotions and actions. That is, the need to belong and to be accepted by a group is powerful. As a user of power words and phrases, you need to tap into that human need occasionally.

And so, if we care about the group, we care about its short-term and long-term reputation. How will this group that we care so much about be remembered? Are the group's goals and deeds shortsighted and self-serving, and if so, will the group be poorly judged in the long run? If you don't think people care about such things, I suggest you take a look around the next university you visit. The names of donors are on permanent plaques peppered everywhere. People care about their legacy and the judgment of their posterity. Mentioning this concern up front is a nice way to hook your readers.

Example: "How will history judge us? Two or three generations from now, will we be seen as a people who made tough decisions and tackled this national debt? Or will our grandchildren curse us for shackling them with taxes that do little but service the interest on money we owe to other nations?"

Appeal to the Gut

Weak: "It appeals to people's primitive instincts."

Powerful: "It creates a visceral response."

As mentioned a few times before, I'm not one for using big words, and I don't advocate using them for their own sake. But I think the word *visceral* is pretty cool. First of all, many people know what it means, so its use isn't too haughty. And second, it evokes the animal instincts of mankind in a distinctively gritty way that sets it apart from other words.

def•i•ni•tion

Visceral means "not intellectual." It implies a deep primitive or animal-like feeling requiring little or no thought. The impulse to run from danger is a visceral response.

Example: "The purpose of this letter is to suggest that we place the previously cut love scene back into the college play. While the rough kissing sequence is certain to raise an eyebrow or two, the scene creates in an audience the type of visceral response that makes live theater so special."

Pack a Wallop with a Contrast

Weak: "We will turn this situation around."

Powerful: "From the swill of corruption will rise a new fortress of morality-based public service."

As with the "historic crossroads" phrase mentioned earlier, drawing a dramatic contrast brings a lot of punch to an opening line—out of darkness comes light, out of sadness comes newfound hope, and so on. It's nothing new: Jesus used contrasts to gain the attention of his audiences. "Blessed are they that mourn: for they shall be comforted," he said before a large crowd. "Blessed are the meek: for they shall inherit the earth." (Matthew 5:4–5)

One attention-getting attribute about contrasts is they provide the counterintuitive concept. Light drawn from darkness? Meek inheriting the earth? It doesn't make sense until the writer explains it. But before the explanation comes the attention-getting. More on counterintuitive writing later.

Example: "From the swill of corruption that this company, its employees, and its stockholders have had to endure will rise a new fortress—a new corporation—that will evoke the work ethic and values upon which this business was founded 75 years ago."

The Least You Need to Know

◆ A good attention-getter in writing is to begin with an image of extremes or contrasts.

◆ Begin a written message with a hypothetical situation or a magnificent vision of what the future could be.

- Use a metaphor—a comparison that does not use *like* or *as*—to create a striking vision that grabs your readers' attention.

- Portray yourself in your writing as being on your reader's side. Remember that people are innately self-serving.

- Hook your reader by changing the word order of a sentence or adding a commanding word or two.

- Describe decisions and actions in a historical context. Make them all sound monumental.

Chapter 2

Sell the Need

In This Chapter

- ◆ Creating a compelling argument
- ◆ Using smart words and phrases
- ◆ Being proactive when you ask for something in a letter
- ◆ Adding emotion in a way that works

If you want to add some intensity to your written ideas, convince your reader there's a need—something missing or broken—that your ideas fulfill. Many times, if there's no perceived need on the part of the person you're trying to persuade, then your words fall unheeded or discounted. Therefore, consider words and phrases that plainly suggest there's something that others need—maybe something you've got! Whether this thing that you bring to the table is personal and useful, or whether it's a thought-provoking, researched solution to a world problem, present your offer or idea in a powerful way, suggesting that it suits an important, unmet need.

Be Compelling as You Create the Necessity

Weak: "There are good reasons …"

Powerful: "There are compelling arguments …"

So you've got some good reasons why someone should hire you, or why your school district should change its absentee policy, or why your boss should change her overtime formula. Big deal. They all have just-as-good reasons for not changing a thing. At the top of the list: everyone hates change, and your notions translate into more work for other people. However, if you have several "compelling arguments" for why they should hire you or change a policy or offer more overtime, well, *now* you have their attention.

Example: "There are several compelling arguments for taking global warming seriously. First, the problem is striking home as areas in the traditionally water-rich United States dry up. Second, there is now strong scientific and political consensus on the phenomenon of global warming, including recognition that huge icy regions on Earth are melting. And third, ecologists and economists suggest that we're in for decades of worldwide thirst, famine, heightened warfare, and personal hardships if we ignore the problem."

Just Suppose That You Juxtapose

Weak: "When compared to …"

Powerful: "If we juxtapose …"

I'm not a fan of big words, although I do enjoy learning new words and making use of them when opportunities present themselves. One such word seems to give a bigger and bigger bang to my arguments every time I use it to sell a need. The word is *juxtapose*, which is a fancy way of saying "compare." I've heard this word used effectively during animated political and business conversations with my good friend Scott Strine, a district sales manager with Pfizer, Inc. "When juxtaposed with last quarter's numbers," he'll say, "the current stats seem very promising." Now how do you argue with a smart-sounding sentence like that? I have found that the word looks good in written communication as well.

def•i•ni•tion

To **juxtapose** two things means to place them side-by-side. The term comes from the Latin adverb *iuxta,* meaning "near," and the Latin verb *posui,* meaning "to place." It is generally used to describe the comparison of two things by placing them next to each other, as you would, say, two X-ray images.

Example: "If we juxtapose this military campaign with our last one, it's easy to see where *this* campaign is headed: stretched-out supply lines, emboldened insurgents wearing us down, and an invisible enemy— guerrilla warfare with no end in sight. Victory is difficult, if not impossible, to envision. For these reasons, Emperor Bonaparte, I strongly suggest that we pull back our reinvasion of Russia."

Offer Yourself as a Solution

Weak: "What can I do for you?"

Powerful: "What important task do you have that isn't getting done right now?"

To get what you want, you often have to offer something in return. As mentioned before, the thing you offer, if not of monetary value, must at least be something that someone needs. What need can you fill, or what problem can you solve for this person? It's not necessary for you to read her mind: just ask her. What's pressing on her daily life? What worry does she have that your gifts or skills might alleviate? If you have what this person wants (or at least what she thinks she wants), you increase your power and influence.

Example: "Consider me a resource that you can rely on. What important task do you have that isn't getting done right now? What limitation does your organization have? If someone were to remedy that limitation right now, what attributes would that person have? I'd very much like to discuss with you how I might be the one with those attributes and those solutions."

> **Copy and Paste** _____
>
> Whenever you write a letter or essay asking that a wrong be righted, make sure you state specifically the remedy you seek. If your message only points out the error or misdeed, then all you're doing is bellyaching. But if you offer one or two possible solutions, then you're part of the cure. The request, even if written sternly or passionately, comes off as more positive. When providing desired outcomes in your letter, you also imply that a) you'll appreciate the actions of others once they're accomplished, and b) you don't have another whiny complaint waiting in the wings.

Take the Bold Stance

Weak: "Not to be controversial, but ..."

Powerful: "I passionately suggest that ..."

Many people approach a situation or a request not wanting to make waves. That's understandable: no one likes to be around a problem child or a whiner. And today's politically correct climate has, unfortunately, taken the wind out of many of our opinionated sails. However, if you want to encourage an action by identifying need, you might consider the confident and courageous approach when writing about the need. After all, there are a lot of problems out there in the world and in your organization. Deciding to adopt one as your own special project and writing about it to those you hope to influence sets you apart—in a good way—from many, many others. *I strongly suggest we have a problem here.* Oh yeah? Well, maybe you're right. So what's your solution? *Ah, I'm glad you asked. Read on ...*

> **Maximizing Maxim** _____
>
> "The world is full of people who are waiting for someone to come along and motivate them to be the kind of people they wish they could be," observes success expert Brian Tracy (www.briantracy.com). But these people are wrong to think that good things will happen to them through surrogates. Says Tracy: "These people are waiting for a bus on a street where no buses pass."

Example: "I passionately suggest to the township that the zoning for this request is all wrong. XYZ Corporation has submitted its paperwork as if its new entrance were simply a residential driveway. In fact, what they are requesting is an industrial truck entrance in the deepest part of a densely populated, residential neighborhood. The idea of large trucks racing through this area, past young children at school bus stops, makes one pause. I strongly recommend that you and the other members of the council deny this request and ask XYZ Corporation to place its new entrance closer to the main highway."

Shift the Paradigm, but *Don't* Say So

Weak: "The paradigms are shifting."

Powerful: "The solutions in this area have changed so dramatically because the underlying *questions* have changed so dramatically."

Also powerful: "The whole way in which we're approaching this area has changed."

Sometimes a new, interesting word or phrase becomes so overused so quickly that its use turns out to be clichéd or easily mocked. "Basically" is a word that I believe has become overused. "Think outside the box" is almost certainly one of those phrases. And in business and education, we're all being warned about "shifting paradigms." Snicker, snicker, and ho hum!

Highlight and Delete

Don't use complicated words as a way to make yourself seem more intelligent than your reader. Yes, sometimes a 10-dollar word is perfect for the sentence and, in that case, by all means you may show it off. But if using this highly technical or elitist term is an end unto itself, keep it locked away in your intelligent mind. Using big words may only confuse and turn off the person you were hoping to impress.

While the word *paradigm*, in its purest form, means "example," the word in recent decades has come to mean a commonly held way of considering a particular topic or problem. So, for instance, if you invent a car that runs on salt water, you will "shift the paradigm" regarding transportation and energy shortages. That is, you will completely change the way people approach the problem of affordable, eco-friendly travel.

For my money, rather than write the hackneyed phrase of "shifting paradigms" and get snickered at (or ignored), it's more effective and powerful simply to write what one means: the solution is different because the large-scale, fundamental problem has changed.

Example: "I hope you'll consider this bold new way of approaching the problem of property taxes. Because we now know how many homeowners—both young and old—are leaving the state due to these high taxes, the whole way in which we're approaching the area of government funding is changing. Indeed, our solutions are going to have to change dramatically because the underlying *questions* about keeping taxpayers in the state have changed so dramatically."

Be Vain? No. Be Proactive? Yes!

Weak: "I'm the best person for this job."

Powerful: "If you give me this job, here is specifically what I'll make happen for you …"

In each of the cover letters for the last three employment applications I've sent out, I offered my prospective boss a bullet-point list of things I would do were he to give me the job. Did he hire me? Yes. Did he like any of the ideas I offered in that cover letter? Not one! And perhaps rightly so: he had his own list of things for me to accomplish. But that's not the point, is it? The point is that I offered myself to this organization as someone who is innovative and *proactive*.

def•i•ni•tion

The **proactive** person is someone who addresses and handles a problem promptly—often before it's even a problem! The antonym is *reactive*, a condition where, say, a manager spends her entire day reacting to situations instead of setting her own leadership agenda. On the personal level, being proactive means doing things rather than hoping for things to come along.

Example: "If you offer me this position, there are several things I'd like to make happen. First, I'd like to be your go-to person for logistics. I believe I can reduce the cost of your shipping operation. Second, I'd like to be your quality-control expert. During my visit, I noticed that many of the quality checks take place at the point of loading your product onto the truck. I think we can move those checks further back, to good effect, in the process."

Emphasize the Emotional

Weak: "Let's concentrate on results."

Powerful: "Let's focus on the dream."

Did Martin Luther King Jr. offer a composed, point-by-point, well-deliberated argument for challenging bigotry in the United States? No. Instead, he shouted, "I have a dream!" and changed the course of history. Did John F. Kennedy methodically spell out all the scientific advantages this country would acquire by building space travel technology? No. Instead, he asserted, "We choose to go to the moon. We choose to go to the moon and do the other things, not because they are easy, but because they are hard!" And off we soared.

People are much more likely to buy into the things you write—regardless of their logical merit—if you are able to pack lots of emotion into your appeal. Of course, don't avoid the commonsense reasons for making something happen, but emphasize the sizzle over the steak whenever you can.

> **Maximizing Maxim**
>
> Personal-development expert Chris Widener (www.chriswidener.com) suggests that people tend to gravitate to the more passionate arguments rather than to the more logical ones. Says Widener: "People always make a decision with emotion and then justify it with logic."

Example: "Join me, won't you? Let's focus on the dream of having a safe playground in this neighborhood. The land is available, the funding is within reach, and the type of child-safe materials we will use are proven by their use in several similar playgrounds in neighboring towns. A safe park for our children. It's a dream that we can realize with your support. Please vote *yes* in this Tuesday's referendum."

Assume Consent

Weak: "Do you ...?"

Powerful: "To what extent do you ...?"

I'll mention this concept again in Chapter 18. However, it's important enough to bring up now: when you write to someone asking for something, add a few phrases here and there that assume this person's consent. In other words, offer your recommendations in a way that seems to take for granted that your idea is a fantastic one and that this person is going to say yes.

Instead of writing, "So, whadda ya say?," write something like, "So, here's how this might work." Or perhaps something like, "What things might you need from our department to help make this happen?" Sure, a strong-minded person can always respond with, "But I didn't say yes yet, did I?" However, by intertwining the presumption of approval throughout your writing, you plant a seed that wasn't there before.

Example: "This is an idea that seems to hold promise. To what extent do you see your department supporting it? What resources are you able to provide, and what resources do you need from me? I look forward to learning your thoughts."

Hurry, This Chapter Is Running Out!

Weak: "We need to do this promptly."

Powerful: "Time is running out."

People are more likely to act—and act sooner—if they believe there's some urgency. And yet, interestingly, they don't always respond to suggestions that urgencies exist—suggestions such as, "Uh, folks, we've got this urgency here." Fortunately, within people's quirkiness, you will discover a quirky predictability: people *do* respond to other written indications, such as those involving scarcity. In other words, they're more likely to make a move toward an action if they think time or resources (or desired prizes) are running out. Just look at ads on television or in newspapers. *While supplies last! One-Day-Only Sale!* Is it *really* worth getting up at 6 A.M. to get to the electronics store just to save $100 on a new laptop? Probably not, but the scarcity ad in the local paper worked on my wife and me last holiday shopping season.

Example: "We have a narrow window of opportunity right now, and time is running out. If we don't make a decisive move within the next week, we will have missed a rare chance to gain a tactical advantage over our competitors."

The Least You Need to Know

◆ Formulate a compelling argument to convince people that you have an effective solution to their problem.

◆ Be proactive and ask probing questions to determine a need or problem and then communicate how you can successfully provide the correct solution.

◆ Appeal to readers emotionally to generate enthusiasm and help motivate the action you desire.

◆ Structure your writing to suggest presumed approval when offering solutions.

Put the Bottom Line Up Front

In This Chapter

- ◆ Getting attention with upfront assertions
- ◆ Being counterintuitive
- ◆ Personalizing your thoughts
- ◆ Writing letters on paper when necessary
- ◆ Instantly getting the reader on your side

Years ago, the United States Army concluded that its internal documents, memoranda, and operations orders were so polluted with verbose sentences that many of them were beyond comprehension. Apparently, some officer had determined decades earlier that the more complicated and condescending he could make something sound, the higher he'd move up the chain of command. Apparently it worked for him—and thousands of other officers over the years had followed suit!

One problem: when no one can understand a U.S. Army operations order, the operation is a disaster. Acknowledging the problem, in 1984 the Army decided that a more straightforward approach to writing (called the Army Writing Style) was in order.

Well, if anyone's going to write for power, it's going to be the Army, right? The two key points to the Army Writing Style are 1) you need to put your bottom line up front (hence the Army acronym BLUF), and 2) you need to use the "active voice" over the "passive voice," a notion also covered in Part 4. Let's look at several words and phrases that help you put your bottom line up front. That is, let's consider some statements that help you quickly and effectively get to the point.

Offer Your Point with Humility

Weak: "I think ..."

Powerful: "In my humble opinion ..."

Much power writing is argumentative writing. In other words, when you write to influence, you're often trying to change someone's mind—not always an easy prospect. And it's tougher still if you come across as arrogant. When you write, "I think that," you're indirectly writing, "The opinion that *everyone* should have is that ..."

If you're going to make an assertion, it pays to begin from the point of humility. Beginning with phrases such as "I might be wrong" or "In my humble opinion" lets the other person know that you're approaching your argument with an open mind and that you're not adamant in your ways. By conveying such flexibility, you remove all kinds of mental barriers to your opinion.

Example: "In my humble opinion, the United States should do away with daylight savings time. It currently makes up a very small portion of the year, making it hardly worth all the confusion. Furthermore, it translates into children waiting at the bus stop in the dark—an unsafe situation."

State Your Fix Right Away

Weak: "Here's why I'm complaining."

Powerful: "Here is the specific resolution I'm looking for."

In your complaint letter or argumentative essay, write as early as possible what remedy to the problem would make you happy. I suggest you place this possible solution somewhere in your opening paragraph.

Many times, when reading such letters or articles, I find myself saying, "Yeah, yeah, so what are you trying to say?" The person has already sold me on the point or the need, so what is he asking for? If I have to go skimming down the page looking for it, I might not be as willing to grant the request or concede the point.

By stating your proposed remedy up front, you allow the reader to consider your supporting points in the context of what you're requesting. If the reader agrees with you right away, he may go about the task of meeting your request, as opposed to placing your letter in an IN box full of stuff.

Example: "Here is the specific resolution I'm looking for: your company should replace the appliance with a new one free of charge, or you should refund the cost of the item and its installation."

Use the Quintessential Thesis Sentence

Weak: "I will now describe why A is B."

Powerful: "A is B because 1, 2, and 3."

Along the lines of asking for a particular outcome right from the start, it pays to delineate the main point and supporting reasons of your argument very early in your message.

You really can't go wrong with the uncomplicated *thesis sentence* format. "Item A is good/bad/true/false because of this, that, and the

def•i•ni•tion

A **thesis sentence** is a sentence that tells your reader the main point you are making and introduces the evidence you'll be using to back it up. It generally appears very early in your letter or essay and often maps out how you're going to make your case.

other thing." By including such a sentence early on, you allow readers to know what's coming up and, in any given paragraph, where they are in your proposal.

State your point, offer three reasons that support your point, and then, following your thesis sentence, go about the task of explaining (or expanding upon) each reason.

Example: "Gentlemen, giving your wives a foot massage each and every night is vitally important because their feet have been working hard all day, because their feet have been cramped in uncomfortable shoes all day, and because lovingly kneading and rubbing their toes and feet will make them appreciate you on an entirely different level."

Start Against the Grain

Weak: "Up means up."

Powerful: "Sometimes, up means down!"

There's a funny thing about common sense: it may be common, but it doesn't always make a lot of sense. For example, "common sense" dictates that the best food diets should be low in fat and high in carbohydrates. Unfortunately, people on such diets are in a constant state of hunger and mental turmoil, and they have a funny way of getting off these diets—by bingeing and therefore regaining much or all of the lost weight. But every generation or so, a doctor such as William Banting or David Jenkins or Robert Atkins comes along and says, "No, keep the carbs down and the fat up." The counterintuitive idea is that fast-digesting foods—and not fatty foods—are what pack the weight on. Over the decades, the low-carb diet has gained considerable respect from scientific and medical researchers.

Let's face it: just because everybody believes in leprechauns doesn't make them real—and a heck of a lot of people believe in leprechauns! Sometimes, for dramatic effect, you need to say, "Uh, maybe there's no such things as leprechauns." You're sure to create a stir, and eventually you might win the debate and gain loads of influence (and a pot of gold, if not one at the end of the rainbow).

Being counterintuitive doesn't necessarily mean being a troublemaker. Many academic and medical research journal editors—not exactly the rabble-rousing types—won't even consider publishing someone's research these days unless it presents a contrarian view. That is, research has the most influence when it makes us challenge what we thought we already knew. The same goes for powerful writing.

Example: "Sometimes up means down. For example, usually when prices go up, consumer resistance goes up—and sales decrease. But counterintuitively, what we have found is that when we raise the price of our fine wines, consumer interest in them—and the assumption of high quality—goes up as well. Lower prices, more resistance. Higher prices, lower resistance. Yes, sometimes up means down!"

Speak Well of the Letter

Weak: "I'm sorry to have to put this in a letter."

Powerful: "I've been thinking about writing this letter for a long time. It seems like the right thing to do."

If you're writing a letter in place of facing someone you'd rather not face, letter-writing expert Samara O'Shea suggests that you not apologize for the letter but instead praise the letter as the right vehicle for what you have to say. Written letters allow you to take an hour to think over what might be embarrassing when blurted out in one minute.

In her book *For the Love of Letters* (HarperCollins, 2007), O'Shea notes that some letters, such as good-bye letters, provide a powerful sense of closure and regaining "control of your emotional state." So why apologize for it? Instead, state up front that you're glad you're putting it in writing.

> **Copy and Paste**
>
> Don't leave a phone message if you have the time to write a letter. Samara O'Shea suggests that ink, paper, and time provide concrete proof of your thoughts. "It's the time you take to choose your words," she says, "that becomes a tangible testament to how much the other person means to you (or how angry you are, which is still a verification of how much he or she means to you)."

So again, don't express regret over the letter. Instead, celebrate it in the letter itself as the way you want the recipient to know what's up.

Example: "I've been thinking about writing this letter for a long time. It seems like the right thing to do. The truth is the more we try to find that certain spark that will keep us together, the more obvious it seems that we'll never find it. It's time for us to separate."

Use the I-Message

Weak: "You're a bonehead for doing that."

Powerful: "I feel upset when you act that way because it seems to make the people we're with uncomfortable."

Clinical psychologist and communications expert Thomas Gordon (who passed away in 2002) is most famous for his Parent Effectiveness Training (PET) program and for his clever invention, the I-message. Gordon suggests that when you use "I" instead of "you" when confronting people, you help prevent their tendency to become automatically defensive (and therefore defiant).

Gordon's I-message has three parts: "I feel _____ (your feelings) when you _____ (the other person's behavior) because _____ (the effect the behavior has on you or a particular situation)."

> **Maximizing Maxim** _____
>
> I-message creator Thomas Gordon suggested that effective communication carries over into the workplace with good management: "Leaders should create the conditions in which all the members feel safe to communicate their ideas and feelings."

Directly addressing the impact of another's actions is mentioned again in Part 2, but it is such a commanding way of putting the bottom line up front in one's writing that it needs to be mentioned here. As I said to my editor, "It hurts me when you tell me the I-message can't go in Part 1 because omitting it seems to diminish the impact of Chapter 3."

Example: "I feel hurt when you walk away from me while I'm in the middle of a sentence because it looks as if you never cared to begin with."

Kill a Tree Every Now and Then

Weak: An e-mail saying, "Thanks."

Powerful: A handwritten letter or card saying, "Thanks."

Allow me to offer a strong endorsement for the handwritten thank-you note. Granted, this book is more about the words than delivery. However, the power of the handwritten "thank-you" note is so strong that it would be folly not to mention it. When you write a quick thank-you note and mail it, you set yourself apart from nearly everyone else. The next time you walk into a card store or a bookstore, check the dust on the boxes of small thank-you notes: they're definitely not flying off the shelves. Blow the dust off and buy a box or two.

Copy and Paste

If anyone spends more than 15 minutes of time on you outside of his or her normal daily work duties, then you should send that person a thank-you note. Such events include job interviews, mentoring, addressing a payroll problem, and tending to a project while you're on vacation.

I keep thank-you stationery in my car. Whenever someone takes extra time or effort in helping me, I note his or her name, write the thank-you note as soon as I leave the establishment, and pop it in the mail. If it's an entry-level customer-service person, I send the thank-you to his or her supervisor: the supervisor appreciates it, and it increases the odds of this employee moving up to a position of greater responsibility.

And speaking of employment, the next time you interview for a job, use this tactic. If a manager talks to 10 prospective employees for a job, odds are you'll be the only one who will send a thank-you. Will it give you the job? No. But in a crowded field of candidates, it more than likely will bring your file to the top for a second look. If it comes down to hiring one of two equally qualified people, the boss is apt to remember the person who showed enough professionalism and courtesy to write "thanks."

Example: "Dear Mr. Bosstoobee, just a quick note of thanks for taking the time to interview me for the position of assistant manager. I hope you'll find me a good match for your organization, and I look forward to the possibility of being a part of your team. Best wishes, Betty Hiresmee."

Use Your Power for Someone Else

Weak: "The subject of this e-mail is Joe Smith."

Powerful: "I am writing to you on behalf of Joe Smith, whom I believe is being treated unfairly."

While on the subject of paper-only letters, it's also worth mentioning the benefit of typing the occasional letter on behalf of someone else who could use some support. As that web-slinging superhero's uncle once noted, with great power comes great responsibility. Why not take some of the great stuff in this book and, from time to time, use it for the benefit of people who can't help themselves?

Highlight and Delete

If you're truly looking for results and control over someone, as opposed simply to venting your complaints and emotions, don't include accusations or insults in your letter to that person. Can you imagine reading an insulting letter and saying, "Hmmm, she has a point— maybe I'll do it her way!"?

There may or may not be such a thing as karma. But there is, without dispute, a certain permanence to the paper letter. If, years from now, someone offers you a life-changing favor, don't be surprised, while you're thanking him, if he takes out from his office desk an old, yellowed letter you wrote on his behalf and that you had long forgotten about.

Example: "Dear Governor, I'm writing to you on behalf of Ahnest Face, an alleged crime suspect who has been secretly held without charges for the last six months in your state prison. While I respect the State's desire for justice and its desire to keep communities safe from such crimes, I appeal to your love for America, where people aren't locked up without being formally charged or without having access to an attorney. As of this writing, Mr. Face's family isn't even sure where he's being kept, other than through news leaks from security guards at the state prison ...."

Take Credit for the Upfront Point

Weak: "It would be a good thing if ..."

Powerful: "I believe we should ..."

As mentioned before, sometimes it's good to keep people focused on the big picture or the group's vision and goals. But remember that power and influence often mean taking credit for things. Of course, you could take credit for other people's ideas: history is loaded with famous people who became that way by stealing someone else's ingenuity. But let's instead assume you're honest. If the upfront idea, observation, or recommendation is yours and you stand to acquire some influence if it gains traction, put the word *I* somewhere in the sentence that introduces it.

In this age of perpetual responsibility shirking and butt protecting, it's refreshing when someone steps up to the plate with an idea she's willing to call her own and is willing to be accountable for. When you add personal ownership to an argument, it gains steam.

Example: "I believe we should go with this new system for calculating the depreciation of our equipment. It allows for a bigger upfront write-off, it's legal, and it's recommended by several accountant colleagues of mine."

Appeal to the Warm Glow of Others

Weak: "Do you have some information that could help me?"

Powerful: "What is the secret to your success?"

When you compliment someone before asking for advice or information, you make that person instantly feel good inside—physiologically so—and therefore more likely to provide what you need, whether it be information or a service or action.

There's a feeling, a warm glow effect, we all get from offering our time or resources to someone else in a charitable way. Psychologist Ulrich Mayr and economists Bill Harbaugh and Daniel Burghart recently conducted studies showing that this isn't just touchy-feely nonsense: there is actually neural activity in the pleasure centers of our brains giving us that warm feeling. And the more voluntary the giving, the greater the neural activity! By giving a compliment, you create the beginning of a warm glow effect that might just lead to you getting what you want or need from the recipient.

Don't be phony in your compliment. For example, don't write that someone is astonishingly organized when she's not. If there's some worthwhile information that you seek, link a truthful, appropriate compliment to that information.

Example: "Dear Chef DeeLish, I've been eating at your restaurant for years, and I can't quite put my finger on the combination of spices over your famous baked shark. What is the secret to your success? What makes this particular dish so special and so celebrated across this tri-state area?"

Tell 'Em They Possess the Gift

Weak: "You're making mistakes."

Powerful: "You've got what it takes to make this right."

Along the same lines of paying a compliment at the beginning of your written request, you're most likely to hold sway over someone if you tell him that he's got what it takes to make something wrong turn right.

There's more about convincing people they're wrong in Part 2, but I can't emphasize enough that the phrase "you're wrong" is the weakest tool for doing so. Putting people on the defensive, in either written or spoken form, might win you a few "zinger" points, but it won't get you what you want, and it will ultimately diminish your influence over them.

Example: "And so, Mr. Mayor, please reconsider my heartfelt request that you open up Narrow Street to all soccer-family parking on Saturdays. I've seen you at the games, and I know you love kids and have several of your own. Plus, I've seen you in action when it comes to issues like this one. Clearly, you've got what it takes to make this right."

The Least You Need to Know

◆ Stating the problem, its causes, and your proposed solution right away is the best way to begin a written argument.

◆ Arguments that catch people's attention often go against the grain.

◆ In some cases, nothing is better than a letter written on paper and placed in the mail.

◆ Use the word *I* to dramatize how something is affecting you and to take personal ownership of your argument and its solution.

◆ Take credit for your ideas, but approach them from a standpoint of humility.

◆ Begin your written request with a sincere compliment and an appeal to the person's generosity.

Chapter 4

Close the Deal

In This Chapter

- ◆ Concluding your case on a strong note
- ◆ Appealing to your reader's innate needs
- ◆ Literary tools that pack a punch
- ◆ Avoiding clichés and other no-no's
- ◆ Petitioning your reader's sense of worth

If a clever hook at the beginning of your message convinces the reader to read on, then a powerful thought or two at the end brings your case to a strong close.

Power words make great literary bookends for what you write. Although they're perfectly fine throughout your essay, these expressions work best at the beginning and at the end to help persuade others about the wonderfulness of your ideas.

Swaying people without getting them to act sometimes isn't any more powerful than dissuading them from acting or keeping them indifferent. Your powerful conclusion needs to close the deal and prompt your readers to action.

For He's a Jolly Good Fellow

Weak: "Do this because it's the right thing to do."

Powerful: "This deed will certainly reflect the fairness and righteousness you've shown in the past."

It's tough to define right and wrong for other people. Your right might be someone else's wrong. Indeed, if we all possessed the same defining set of virtues, there wouldn't be debates, arguments, or war. And there wouldn't be much of a need for quality argumentative writing; the appropriate course of action would already be apparent.

However, if you refer to what someone else once *thought was* right in your quest to convince him what *now is* right, well, now you've got something. A good way to conclude an argument is to remind a person what he, himself, had once championed. Remind him about the righteousness you have observed in him in the past. Prompt him to draw out that goodness once again.

Example: "Thank you again for considering our neighborhood's request for a zoning change. You have a great reputation for keeping large-scale business construction out of the beautiful neighborhoods of this county. We hope you'll do the same for our neighborhood. Your approval of this zoning change will certainly reflect the fairness and righteousness you've shown in the past."

Emphasize the Acceptable Amount of Unacceptability

Weak: "It's slightly inconsistent."

Powerful: "There's an acceptable amount of variance."

Don't wrap up your persuasive writing by drawing attention to its drawbacks or its possible inaccuracies. Of course, in a long case study–type of essay, you want to mention the downside of your argument, the potential for measurement errors, and alternative solutions. And, systematically, you want to address them and explain why your argument and your evidence override those obstacles. However, as you conclude your argument, play up your case and play down the downside. As there is no such thing as a perfect solution, it is up to you to sell the good solution with an acceptable degree of variance.

The variance of something is how much it differs from something else. In quality control, variance is how much something deviates from the perfect specifications that define it. In all types of professional work, there is an acceptable variance.

This is especially so when dealing with minor inaccuracies within your research. There is always the possibility that the numbers you have come up with could be obtained through other, inaccurate means—even through random chance! In social science experiments, if there's a 5-in-1,000 chance that the numbers you've come up with could have happened randomly, that's considered an acceptable amount of variability. There are computer programs that help define variance, but that's another topic for another time.

For now, know that as you deal with alternatives to your findings and your solution, you should play them down as "acceptable variation" and "acceptable dissenting opinion" as you bring your argument to a powerful close.

Example: "Once again, we hope you'll select our company to manufacture your widgets. Even with the implementation of all the cost-cutting measures you've requested, there is only a miniscule (but exceedingly acceptable) amount of variance in your product off our assembly lines. With our low cost, high uniformity, and daily dependability, it makes sense to have us as your sole supplier."

Readdress the Need

Weak: "We should join this organization because everyone is doing it."

Powerful: "Joining this organization will give us access to important information."

My town has two competing cable TV companies. I occasionally receive visits from door-to-door salespeople trying to convert me from the other guys to their company. Generally, I'm not very nice to them, especially when I'm writing. But I often find myself talking to the salesperson who begins with, "What's your cable company *not* giving you that maybe *we* might be able to?" And the salesperson who finishes his pitch by emphasizing this need will, in all likelihood, one day get my business.

Make sure you hit the reader with the same thing at the end of your message that prompted that reader to keep reading at the beginning. Emphasize how your solution addresses a need that that reader has.

Highlight and Delete

Although the "me, too" argument carries a certain amount of influence, don't ever rely too heavily on the "everybody's doing it" argument. When large investment banks in the United States crumbled in recent years under the weight of the inferior mortgage loans they had funded, there were undoubtedly executives explaining behind closed doors: "But everyone was doing it." Sometimes the boards of directors listened; often they didn't.

Remember the salesperson's creed: no need, no sale. That's not to say people won't ever do things for you unless there's something in it for them. But if your goal is to motivate people to take an action that has an impact on both them and the people around them, pointing out an unmet need is the best way to make it happen.

Example: "The thing I like about this professional organization is that, on a monthly basis, it reveals to its members what contractors such as ourselves should be charging for very specific types of jobs. Therefore, the next time we put out a bid, we won't be doing so blindly. Joining this organization will give us access to this important information."

Mention the Expert

Weak: "Lots of people like the idea."

Powerful: "Joe de Expert likes the idea."

If everyone else were jumping off a cliff, would you jump off, too? Okay, maybe that's a poor rhetorical question: a lot of psychological research out there suggests that many a person *would* jump. But there are plenty of strong-minded people out there, especially moms, who are less persuaded by the "everybody's doing it" argument.

However, these people *do* respect the opinions of experts, and they will give the expert opinion at least some consideration. If 4 out of 5 dentists like your idea, then concluding your recommendation with that fact is a nice way to drive home your point.

Example: "I strongly recommend that we expand our sales force and reduce the size of the territory each salesperson covers. Joe de Expert, our company counterpart on the West Coast, likes the idea. He says, in such a rapidly expanding market, keeping the sales force as is will ultimately send too much business over to our competitors."

Mention Value

Weak: "It is necessary."

Powerful: "It adds value."

The term *value* can be approached from many different categories: economics, morality, personal worth, community standards, and so on. The good news is that when a word has a positive connotation in so many different ways, you can use that word to your advantage whenever you're winding up an essay.

The idea of "value added" stems from economics. If you perform an action and the action increases the asking price of your product, then there's value added. But telling readers that something adds value might also mean that it adds value to their lives or to their feeling of goodness or purpose.

Writing that something is necessary is, well, not very convincing. "If it's so necessary," asks the reader, "then why am I doing just fine without it?" But if you tell the reader that something adds value to the situation, then you've gone a little further in convincing her to make the move.

Example: "Adding this new filter onto the engines we manufacture isn't simply necessary for meeting EPA standards. Doing so adds values in several ways. First, by adding these filters, we can advertise ourselves, appropriately so, as a 'green' company. And second, our marketing people tell us that we can increase the price of our engines by $200, while the filter itself—including labor—is costing us only $100."

Know That People Value Time and Money

Weak: "Let's run things more efficiently."

Powerful: "Let's save some time!"

Along the lines of bringing up value, you might also mention how your idea will save time and money. The word *efficiency* is a bit coat-and-tie and doesn't pack much of an emotional wallop. But people love their time and they love their money, and they respond positively to the idea of adding to either one.

Appeal to people's desire for more time or money by bringing up how your idea saves one or the other or both. Oh, your idea doesn't save either one? Hmmm, well, in that case go back to the "adds value" phrase, mentioned previous.

Example: "We're all overworked and stressed out. I suggest we scrap the daily close-of-business meeting and switch to a weekly department meeting. Let's save some time. Let's hit the ground running in the morning by being able to clear some work off our desks at the end of each day."

Remind Someone You're Counting on Her

Weak: "You're in charge. Now get it done."

Powerful: "Folks have entrusted you with this responsibility. Don't let them down."

If you write to a person, "Hey, you're the person in charge—make something happen, for goodness' sake," you'll probably generate a response. But it's unlikely to be the response you want. First, if the person is inclined to address your letter, she's probably not *really* in charge. And if she is in charge, your sharp words are prone to make her defensive and indifferent.

Instead, offer her the side compliment of reminding her that people have respected her enough to place her in a position of authority. And remind her that those same people are counting on her to do right by them. Appeal to her ego and to her sense of responsibility to the group for which she's answerable.

Example: "When this town put you in that job, we all celebrated. There was a warm feeling out there—a feeling that you would bring new ideas and a new decency to the job and set things straight. Folks have entrusted you with this responsibility. Don't let them down. We're counting on you, and we know you'll do us right."

At the End of the Cliché ...

Weak: "At the end of the day ..."

Powerful: "Our guiding principle (or overriding goal) ..."

"At the end of the day" is one of those phrases that seems to get weaker and weaker as it becomes more and more overused. The phrase essentially means "after all the evidence has been examined," but it seems to be used more these days to mean "after examining what's important and what's not."

A good friend of mine, John Greene—a unique military officer with combat experience in both the U.S. Army and U.S. Air Force—despises the "end of the day" phrase as too *cliché* and too unclear. "If some principle is important at the end of the day," he asks rhetorically, "why shouldn't it be important throughout the day?" But, notes Greene, that notion doesn't stop military officers from using the phrase all the time.

def•i•ni•tion

> A **cliché** is a saying that it so overused that its use is more embarrassing than clever. An example is: "Never in my wildest dreams ...." The word *cliché* may be used as an adjective as well. Something that's clichéd is unoriginal.

Instead of using this tired, confusing phrase, try something that is stronger and more straightforward—something like "our overriding goal" or "our unwavering principle." At the end of the day, you'll take your shoes off and thank yourself.

Example: "Of course it would be financially beneficial to turn these people away. But our organization's guiding principle, carrying us for 75 years, is we will bring no harm to others, and that we will extend a hand whenever one is asked for."

Repeat a Phrase

Weak: "Please consider these recommendations."

Powerful: "Let's ... Let's ... Let's ..."

Why do some songs resonate in our minds, possibly for a lifetime? The reason goes back to the caveman days. Apparently, there's something in the human brain that responds favorably to the repetition of sound. Caveman music? Banging the same sequence of beats over and over again on the drums. If you think about it, the biggest hits on the radio often follow this model by repeating the same beat, the same refrain, or the same keywords over and over.

Repeating a phrase works nicely in speeches, too, such as Martin Luther King's "I have a dream," Ronald Reagan's "facts are stubborn," or Barack Obama's "yes, we can."

But don't restrict this clever literary device to songs or speeches. Use the power of repeating some phrases in your writing to create a nice parallelism and to level your argument. "People desire integrity in their leaders. People desire empathy in their leaders. And people desire effectiveness in their leaders." A lot of unnecessary words? Maybe. But the energy and the intensity of the repetition almost certainly outweigh the "extra" words.

Example: "Let's look forward to a new era in political honesty and accountability. Let's say no to the good ol' boys' club that's been doing business in the state capitol for the last 40 years. Let's make a difference. Let's elect Joey Crooked for State Senator!"

Add the Element of Fear

Weak: "Here's a potential risk."

Powerful: "Here's what you should be afraid of."

If you want someone to stop doing something, don't mention the action's potential risk. The reader's likely internal response: "Well, it hasn't hurt me so far." Instead, trigger the person's sense of fear, especially if the fear is warranted.

People desire a sense of security and safety, so much so that they're often willing to give up a lot of other things to gain that feeling. Psychologist Abraham Maslow suggested decades ago that security was right up there with food and sex on the human "needs" priority. So if you suggest to someone that his security is threatened, you lean him in your desired direction.

Don't bore the reader with levels of risk. Shock him into action with the frightening reality of what will happen if he doesn't change his ways.

Highlight and Delete

Don't forever be an alarmist in your writing. Eventually, your warnings will become numbing to your readers and the impact of your words will wane. Instead, offer the occasional upbeat essay about the person who saw a problem, implemented a solution, and made a difference.

Of course, it's worth noting that you don't want to make things up or overdramatize a threat. That might pack a one-time punch, but you'll never convince the person about anything again. On the other hand, if a threat is real, and it might prompt someone into action, don't be shy about mentioning it and playing it up. Sometimes people need to be jolted into doing the right thing.

Example: "Here's what you should be afraid of: if you do nothing and these beasts come out of the woods and start roaming residential neighborhoods, you'll be responsible for whatever these animals do to your children or to the children of your friends. I strongly suggest that now is the time to set up traps or send out hunting parties."

Offer Limited Choices

Weak: "And so, darling, may we buy a sports car?"

Powerful: "And so, darling, would you prefer a Porsche or a Corvette?"

I've mentioned how assuming the consent of the reader is a powerful way to present an argument. Let's take it a step further. If you assume that the reader is agreeing with you, then you also assume that the options you're presenting to her fall in line with her agreeing with you. For example, if she agrees with you, then you're not going to present any of the "no" alternatives to your proposal.

Admittedly, offering limited options falls under the rhetorical fallacy of providing a false dilemma. However, a false dilemma is more "do this or the world will end." Offering two or three righteous options that fall under the umbrella of your larger recommendation is an effective sales tactic that helps you wrap up your suggestion with a punch.

Example: "This nonconfrontational letter is intended to broach the topic without fighting and without emotion. I've worked all my life for the opportunity to buy a nice car, and I truly hope that, as my wife, you'll cheer on my bringing this dream to reality. And so, darling, would you prefer a Porsche or a Corvette?"

The Least You Need to Know

◆ At the end of your written argument, emphasize how your suggestion will bring about something that the reader currently lacks.

◆ Finish your recommendation by accentuating its positive points.

◆ Appeal to your reader's desire to save time, money, and aggravation.

◆ Expert endorsement, value added, appeal to security, and repeated keywords are all persuasive written tools.

◆ Avoid clichés.

◆ Appeal to people's ego, sense of worth, and sense of responsibility.

Part 2

Power Words for Persuading

Being assertive often means speaking up for yourself without seeming too pushy, mean-spirited, or self-serving. It's not always a comfortable undertaking, but once you learn to do it effectively, having your say becomes effortless and empowering.

Often, understanding power means understanding corroboration. That is, it's easier to gain and maintain power when others allow you to have it and hold it. People are more likely to work with you or provide what you need when you use your words to help them feel good about themselves or their contributions.

Your words may become your trademark. People enjoy listening to you, and your branded words make them remember you in a positive way. Finally, the right power word allows you, in an instant, to spice up the appeals you make to others. Power doesn't end with the spoken word, but, more often than not, it begins there.

Frame Your Words in a Big Picture

In This Chapter

- ◆ Appealing to what people cherish
- ◆ Knowing when to be specific, and when not to
- ◆ Speaking in active voice
- ◆ No-nonsense corniness
- ◆ Making people feel good about themselves
- ◆ Appealing to people's love for their team or their good cause

There's a reason why politicians get a lot of mileage out of topics such as national security, jobs, and gas prices: these items are part of the national "big picture," and therefore each voter can relate to them. When your words pertain to the big picture, they resonate.

If you can voice your assertions in ways that apply to a collective goal, philosophy, or passion, you'll have a much easier time gaining the power you seek.

Recall That Great Pioneer

Weak: "Let's keep in mind the philosophy of our organization."

Powerful: "Our actions must forever answer the question, 'What would John de Founder do?'"

So your organization has an overriding philosophy of reducing cost, and you mention it in your presentation on cost savings. Blah, blah, blah. If you notice any glazed looks on people's faces, it's because they've heard it all before and there's no passion in your argument.

However, if you invoke the name of your organization's revered founder, you might notice a bit more energy and nodding heads in the room. What have you done? You've drawn out the big-picture ideals that the founder stood for. You have added a venerated face to your case.

When a Christian asks, "What would Jesus do?" or a Republican asks, "What would Reagan do?" it's neither clichéd nor superficial: these folks truly pine for a time when people rallied around the face of ground-breaking leadership. By bringing the name of a great founder into play, you appeal to the emotions of your group and make them listen.

Maximizing Maxim

The point of the phrase "What would Jesus do?"—or others like it—is to consider someone generally viewed as a savior or sovereign and make him more of a model for everyday living. Charles Sheldon, commonly attributed as the founder of the phrase, wrote in the late 1890s that the model of greatness could be applied to mundane actions. For example, in his book *In His Steps* (Bridge-Logos, reprint 2000), Sheldon writes of an unemployed businessman who seeks to "begin again and work up to a position where he could again be to hundreds of young businesspeople an example of what Jesus would and could do in business."

Example: "We need not alter our value set or our philosophy in light of this recent crisis. All we need to do is ask, 'What would John de Founder do?' And our actions, as they have in the past in so many wonderful ways, must mirror the answer to that paramount question."

Make the Guarantee Super-Specific

Weak: "This plan will improve productivity."

Powerful: "This plan will increase the output of each worker by 40 percent."

As you're presenting an idea to your boss, your group of bosses, or your team, don't be surprised to find a few sets of eyes glazing over. It's no wonder: they've heard it all before. If you're making claims about time savings, cost savings, or increased productivity, it's to be expected. A proposal that doesn't offer one of those things isn't likely even to be brought up.

Fight the daydreaming of your audience by making your projections very specific, involving detailed, quantitative support. Does your proposal save money? Big deal. But does it save $7,413.87 per year for each and every employee in your organization? Wow! You just woke up your audience!

Example: "These new ergonomic chairs will allow our employees to move around without having constantly to stand up and reposition themselves. Our study suggests that new hydraulic rolling chairs will increase the output of each worker by 40 percent."

Keep It Active

Weak: "It has been decided that ..."

Powerful: "I have decided that ..."

Remember how the army (mentioned in Chapter 3) decided to improve its communications by using the active voice? The decision-makers knew the active voice is direct, and that using the active voice gives the writer or speaker ownership of the ideas. Influential people own their decisions—popular or otherwise—and converse in the active voice. Instead of saying, "The decision has been made," the powerful person says, "I have made this decision."

There are plenty of reasons for weak-minded people to hide behind their decisions or to pretend as if the decisions are not theirs at all. If someone is able to portray a new idea as a group-contrived effort, then he can insert himself inside the group if things don't go as planned. That may keep him around for a bit longer, but it's also going to remove any influence he may have had in the past.

It's not a comfortable thing to say, and, of course, if you say it a bit too gleefully, you'll sound power-hungry. But if you can own your decisions and maintain a sense of humility at the same time, people will respect you and be likely to follow your lead.

Example: "After discussing with each of you your concerns about the new vacation policy, I have decided to place it on hold until after the summer. There's no reason why our peak vacation season, and the vacations themselves, need to be overshadowed by stress and hard feelings over what might just be some misunderstanding over a new procedure."

Win One for the Gipper

Weak: "Give it your all!"

Powerful: "Do it for the team!" (or "Do it for the cause!")

When you say to someone, "Do your best" (or something similar), you might be unintentionally implying that she doesn't always offer her finest work. "What does he think?" she might ponder to herself. "Does he think that with his rousing word or two, he's going to motivate me to some higher level of accomplishment? Hmmph!" Asking people to give it their all might (or might not) breed such resentment, but in any event, it's unlikely to inspire the troops. If nothing else, it's too clichéd.

Instead of addressing people's level of performance, why not appeal to their level of commitment? People are very often induced by dedication to their working group or to a lofty cause. That's how leaders rally soldiers before a military operation. Once the battle is underway, they are likely to fight for their comrades, but to get the entire unit moving forward, the commander trumpets the grand, righteous cause.

Example: "Any way you slice it, this town has been very good to us and our children. We need to give something back by supporting this new town center. Call your town councilman. Write letters. Do it for the town!"

> **Maximizing Maxim** _____
> In June of 1944, just before U.S. forces landed in Normandy,
> General Dwight D. Eisenhower celebrated the soldiers' willingness
> to embark in the Great Crusade against the Nazis. "The eyes of liberty
> loving people everywhere march with you," he wrote to them. "The tide
> has turned! The free men of the world are marching together to Victory!"
> Clearly Ike knew how to emphasize the cause over the challenge.

Address the Grand Struggle

Weak: "This is urgent."

Powerful: "This immediately addresses the problem of X."

Simply telling someone that something is important isn't automatically going to convince him that it is so. What's important to you isn't necessarily important to me or anyone else. As mentioned before, just because you get specific doesn't mean that you've forgotten about the big picture.

Address the specific, big-picture problem as you wrap your words around it. Tell the person what difficulty his actions are directly going to tackle. Be explicit. The more precise the problem/action/effect/resolution, the better.

> **Highlight and Delete** _____
> Be wary of defining
> yourself or your organi-
> zation by a particular struggle
> that it faces. Once the chal-
> lenge has been met, the goal
> has been reached, or the
> struggle goes away, you may
> find yourself in a bit of an
> identity crisis.

Example: "Thanks so much for considering this overnight assignment. Replacing that old wiring will immediately eliminate the fire hazard and put everyone's mind at ease. Will you please stay and fix it?"

Talk About Souls per Minute

Weak: "Doing this will save lives."

Powerful: "Our numbers suggest that we'll save one life every six minutes if we operate this new program."

Suppose I were to tell you that I had met Satan and discussed his impressive work ethic. If I were to tell you that Satan gathers many souls per day, you might be impressed and you might not. But suppose I were to tell you that Satan gathers 11,639 souls per minute. Seem more impressive? Sure. That large, nonrounded number is unnerving—perhaps enough to convince someone to behave a little better.

> **Copy and Paste**
>
> Write down the seven things most important to you in this life. Keep them in your mind, and relate one or two of them whenever you're addressing big-picture problems to others. There's a good chance your list is much the same as everyone else's.

The same pertains to saving souls, or at least saving lives (or helping lives). If you suggest that a contribution of money or time will save lives, expect a glazed, unimpressed look. But if you tell them that their effort will save 17 lives, or 3 lives for each hour they work, you may prompt them into action. Remember the television commercials for feeding the poor and hungry overseas? Just $10 would feed, say, seven people for a month. Those were (and still are) very compelling appeals.

Example: "This new filter system within the tunnels will instantly begin removing cancer-causing impurities from the air. One independent study suggests that, over the course of 20 years, this system will save one person from chronic lung disease every six minutes."

Disapprove of the Specific Behavior

Weak: "You are *always* late."

Powerful: "You were late for our meeting today and our scheduled phone call yesterday."

I once complained to my boss about a co-worker. "What's your problem with him?" asked my boss.

"He's always a jerk," I answered.

"Well," my boss hesitated, "what's the specific behavior?" I didn't have one.

"And what specific resolution are you seeking?" my boss asked.

Again, I didn't have one. "Uh, well, I guess I want him to stop always being a jerk," was my weak response.

I hate to admit it, but my boss was right on several counts. First, by suggesting that someone was *always* acting a certain way, my exaggeration weakened my argument. Second, by addressing personalities instead of actions, my complaint couldn't take any form. And finally, by not offering a specific solution to my complaint, I lost my boss's willingness to act.

The truth is, if you complain to someone about a person's mind-set or manner, you're being too vague and perhaps a bit too much of a mind reader. But if you address specific behavior, you are more likely to draw attention to your complaint and, if you're asked for a desired resolution, you'll be able to say, "I want him to stop acting (in this specific way)." That's certainly much more effective than, "I want him to stop thinking the way he does."

Example: "You were late for our meeting today and our scheduled phone call yesterday. Has there been something keeping you from these planned obligations?"

Speak to the Impact

Weak: "Here's what you did wrong."

Powerful: "Here are the adverse results of your actions."

Along the lines of disapproving of a specific behavior, you might garner the attention of someone by pointing out the specific consequences of that behavior. Again, if you address a person's personality trait or behavior, you might be pushing him up against the wall with little choice but to become defensive. On the other hand, if you calmly point out the specific, unpleasant effects of that behavior, the specifics might prompt him to address the problem.

And again, bringing up those adverse results leads fairly easily to discussing a workable remedy. It's much easier to change a result than to change a personality. Before approaching this person, ask yourself: "What is the very specific result of this person's behavior that bothers me? How might that specific thing be changed or done away with to my satisfaction?" And then let that answer form the basis for how you approach the person.

> **Highlight and Delete** _____
>
> Don't address someone's disappointing behavior in front of others. It's humiliating, and that person will forever resent it. If it's a friend or personal companion, it's best to broach the subject behind closed doors. If it's a co-worker or someone who works for you, contact your human resources manager for guidance on the proper way to proceed: one-on-one behind a closed door is often _not_ the way to confront someone at work.

Example: "By falling asleep during your overnight shift, you placed this building in jeopardy. Clearly, if you were asleep, you weren't watching the security monitors, and you weren't walking your rounds."

Be Corny with a Compliment

Weak: "Not bad."

Powerful: "You did 10 times better than anyone else in that situation would have done."

As I mention in my book *The Complete Idiot's Guide to Motivational Leadership*, something that seems overly flattering or corny as you say it doesn't necessarily seem so to the person who hears it. In fact, a syrupy compliment often has a very pleasing ring to the one receiving it.

The following phrases may look corny in print, but they work.

- ◆ "Great job! Keep up the good work."

- ◆ "What a great report. It looks like something in a catalog!"

- ◆ "What a wonderful idea! How'd you come up with it?"

- ◆ "You're smart—what do *you* think of that proposal?"

- ◆ "I'm so proud to be a part of this team."

Example: "Joe, you handled yourself very well in front of that irate customer. You stayed cool and professional 10 times better than anyone else in that situation would have."

Make a Bold (Unprovable) Claim

Weak: "This is a wonderful success story."

Powerful: "Our story is one of the best success stories in the world."

Up until this part of the chapter, I've championed mentioning specific actions and specific results. Now, it's worth giving a nod to the broad-stroke observation or claim. After all, it is the big picture that we're talking about. Right?

Some very motivating boasts sound great but really aren't verifiable. That's okay. If the claim is steeped in truth and, using some type of qualitative measure, might hold merit, try it on for size. If a friend is wearing a very nice dress, what's wrong with saying "That's one of the nicest dresses I've seen this spring!"? If a colleague gives a very good PowerPoint presentation, what's wrong with saying later, "That's one of the most professional presentations I've seen in the last 10 years."? Is it 100 percent accurate? Maybe yes, maybe no—we'll never know. But it will make that person feel very good about herself, and she'll appreciate you for it.

Example: "Our story is one of the best success stories in the world. The idea of taking a company worth only several thousand dollars on paper and turning it into a major producer of repair software is the stuff entrepreneurial dreams are made of."

Remind People of Their Good History

Weak: "Yes, all hell is breaking loose."

Powerful: "We'll get through this—we always have."

Some years ago, as a production manager at a paper mill, I watched as the long, continuous sheet of new wet paper broke and plugged up the paper machine so badly that our crew knew it would take hours to clean up. Hard, sweaty work, and no one was happy.

Fortunately, Dave, my boss, came back to the mill to lend a hand. Instead of jumping in and getting the team hustling, he invited everyone to the break room. He passed out cold drinks, and we all appreciated the rest. Dave told some war stories about all the trouble that old machine had given him over the years.

About 30 minutes later, Dave said, "Well, folks, this is about as bad as it gets. But let's take it slow and safe and help each other out. We'll get through this—we always have."

He was right: as bad as it was, we had all been through it before, and—several hours and many sore muscles later—it had always turned out okay. And so it did that night.

During a particularly bad situation, remind people of their good history of handling adversity. And remind them that if they keep doing the good thing they're doing, this too shall pass.

Example: "Let's not look at this bump in the road as the whole road. It's just one tiny part of a very long stretch. Use the things you've learned in the past and help others who can benefit from your knowledge. We'll get through this—we always have."

The Least You Need to Know

- Appeal to people's love for their patriarch or matriarch.

- Appeal to people's love for their team or their good cause.

- Be very specific about what you promise, what you see wrong, and how you'd like things fixed.

- Don't hide behind your suggestions or decisions. Don't speak in the passive voice.

- With your words, make people feel good about their successes and about themselves.

Chapter 6

Offer Trademark Lines

In This Chapter

- ◆ Finding a catchphrase
- ◆ Using a line to show support
- ◆ Helping people remember you
- ◆ Looking for a solid answer
- ◆ Playing games with words

CBS basketball announcer and commentator Bill Raftery would probably not be very well known were it not for his trademark sayings. After all, analysts calling the games are shown on the screen only once or twice during each game; the true stars of basketball are on the court.

But Raftery gets it: he knows that a catchphrase or two makes a person better remembered. And being well known in any field—as long as professionalism goes with it—translates into power and success. Raftery watched his fellow New Jerseyan Dick Vitale become popular during ESPN's first 10 years using lines such as "It's awesome, baby!" And so, over the last two decades, Raftery has come up with a few memorable ones of his own, such as "With a kiss!" or "Nothing but nylon!"

Don't be goofy or profane. But if you have a phrase that tells it like it is, and you craft it as your own, people will remember you. Your phrased philosophy will, at some point, have an effect on others.

Be a Tad Smarter

Weak: "Of course."

Powerful: "Indeed!"

If you start a sentence off with "of course" or "certainly," you won't gain much attention because everyone tries to punctuate a sentence those two ways. However, it you take it up a notch and use a word such as *indeed, indisputably,* or *irrefutably,* you'll raise an eyebrow or two, and you'll prompt people to listen further. Use that same word often, and it'll become one of your trademarks.

As I've mentioned before, don't use big words for their own sake: it comes off as condescending. For example, *indubitably* is a bit much. But *indeed* is cool because people recognize it even if they don't often use it.

If people walk by you in the hall saying your trademarked word back to you—"Indeed! Indeed!"—it may be a bit of a jab. But more likely, it's the type of recognition and acclaim that comes with celebrity. It's a fun, harmless way of making people take notice of you and focus on your opinions.

Example: "There are compelling reasons we should consider this proposal. Indeed, I believe this idea could change the way we do business with our first-time customers."

Love It, Even If You Hate It

Weak: "This has to get done."

Powerful: "Ya gotta love it, crazy!"

I often tell the story of my commander at U.S. Airborne School, Leonard B. Scott. Throughout all the harassment, the humid runs, the parachute drills, and the muddy drop zones, Scott was there, shouting, "You gotta love it, crazy!" We all laughed at that saying (although certainly not to his face). But it was his trademark, and all these years later, I still remember Colonel Scott's name, professionalism, and catch-phrase. Unlike many colonels I've known, Scott was always on hand, beating us at push-ups, going through the same drudgery we were, and cheering us on every step of the way.

When you're with a group of people muscling through a very difficult task (spring cleaning, store inventory), don't remind them that it has to get done. Instead, say, "Ya gotta love it, crazy!" Have a deranged smile and wide eyes on your face and pretend you're loving every minute of it. It'll break up the drudgery and make those people smile. And the next time you're all undertaking a tough job, don't be surprised if someone looks at you and says, "So, ya gotta love it, crazy!"

Maximizing Maxim

A trademark line that picks people up is more than simply a gimmick. More than 75 years ago, motivational expert Dale Carnegie suggested that if you pretend to be happy and excited about something, you'll not only end up convincing others, but you'll have yourself believing it! Said Carnegie: "Act enthusiastic, and you'll *be* enthusiastic!"

Example: "Ah, clearing a drainage pipe in the pouring rain. The sights, the smells, the labor. There are 100 places I could be besides here right now, but I'd rather spend this time here with you fine people undertaking this grand ordeal. Ya gotta love it, crazy!"

There's Something to This Catchphrase

Weak: "Part of what you're saying is correct."

Powerful: "There's definitely something to that."

Telling someone that she's partially right isn't likely to get her on your side. However, accentuating the part that you agree with, especially through a trademark line, is apt to keep her on your side, even as you enter the touchy subject of what you disagree with.

Why not emphasize that you agree to an extent by saying so with a catchphrase? "Hey, we're halfway there!" "I'm 99 percent on your side with this thing." Sure, the other 1 percent is going to come up, but approaching a discussion from the point of commonality makes for a much more pleasant and productive conversation.

Full disclosure: "There's definitely something to that" is one of my favorite catchphrases, and I use it at least three times every day. Sometimes, when someone is tossing out an idea, she ends it by saying, "Well, Scott, I'll bet you're going to tell me that there's definitely something to that!" She's right: I was just about to!

Example: "There's definitely something to that. You're absolutely correct that the penalty for late papers should be 10 percent off the student's grade per each day late. I'm wondering, however, if you've considered the possibility of a disciplinary consequence as well."

Suggest One Step Back

Weak: "Maybe that wasn't such a good idea."

Powerful: "Let's pursue a return to normalcy."

"Return to normalcy" is a catchphrase from U.S. President Warren Harding, who coined it and used it as a campaign slogan in 1920. The word he meant was probably *normality*, but *normalcy* is kinda cool, and, strictly speaking, *normalcy* was listed in the dictionary even before Harding made it famous.

It's tough to admit that a new plan isn't working, whether it was your idea or someone else's. But if things are going horribly wrong and the situation is upside-down, maybe hearkening back to the earlier, more normal circumstances is worth suggesting.

Highlight and Delete

If you want things to change and change in a hurry, save the blame game for some other time. It's tough, if not impossible, to implement change if everyone's defenses are up. Suggest to the group what needs to happen and, assuming the group buys into the change, wait until after things have settled down to discuss ways to keep the bad times from happening again.

Example: "I respectfully suggest that this additive isn't working in our manufacturing process. It hasn't served as an effective water repellent in our product, and it has created all kinds of slipping dangers and clean-up problems on the production line. Maybe we should pursue a return to normalcy and get rid of it for now."

Get Results

Weak: "Let's try for some good results."

Powerful: "Results! Results! Results!"

When the late Tim Russert, an NBC-TV news anchor, famously predicted that Florida would decide the 2000 presidential election, he wrote on a small dry-marker board, "Florida, Florida, Florida." That word, repeated three times, would become something of a mantra for those describing Russert's political savvy. Russert began to say it himself, even using it to describe other battleground states in later elections. It was a very catchy line and very telling of his forecasting skills.

Instead of asking for results (or productivity or victory or cleanliness or anything else), why not exclaim the word three times? It will get people's attention and, if the line works famously, people will remember you for it. "Profit! Profit! Profit!" This might not be the catchphrase to utter three times an hour: you'll have people hearing it in their nightmares. But if rendered, say, two or three times a week, it sets in, pleasantly, and is remembered.

Example: "People don't care about our catchy slogan or what's in our department store windows or how much our retail prices are marked down at any given second. What they care about is being treated respectfully and being helped when possible. Service! Service! Service!"

Ask the Rhetorical Question

Weak: "Maybe we should do something about that."

Powerful: "If not us, who? If not now, when?"

More than 2,000 years ago, the Jewish philosopher Hillel the Elder said: "If I am not for myself, who will be for me? But if I am *only* for myself, what am I? And if not now, when?" It's a *rhetorical question* that has aged well over the millennia, and the suggestion behind the question—that we all step forward when our brothers and sisters need us—is more pertinent than ever. The world needs more selfless people.

def•i•ni•tion

A **rhetorical question** is essentially a statement formulated as a question. Either no response is expected, or the answer is so obvious that it is not necessary. Rhetorical questions are offered for dramatic effect and not to elicit a reply.

Create a poignant rhetorical question, use it often, and make it yours. Just don't use more than one at a time. A speech, for example, littered with rhetorical questions can be tedious to listen to and more preachy than most people want to handle.

Example: "Having hungry people in our community goes against all that is righteous and humane about America. If we, the citizens of this town, don't act, then who will? And if not now, when people here need it the most, then when?"

Ask the Nonrhetorical Question

Weak: "So, that's what I'm suggesting."

Powerful: "So, when can we get this rodeo a-runnin'?"

Sometimes a pointed question requires no answer—but sometimes it does. A trademark line might be a lighthearted phrase basically asking, "May I get started?"

Some cultures in the world frown upon the abrupt request, especially if it involves a decision with a lot of people attached. But Western cultures generally celebrate the person who's unafraid of asking outright for a decision and, if the decision is yes, for a starting point for time and resources.

"So, when can we start building this popsicle stand?" That's one possibility, and there are hundreds of others. Select one that's funny and disarming and make it your own. Will people at some point start saying it back to you, teasingly? Yes. But at least they know that they're about to be asked for a solid answer.

Example: "It seems to me that five years without changing our standard operating procedure is way too long. We all know these rules were based on several notions that simply don't apply anymore. As a result, many of the steps we follow are either unnecessary or pointing us in the wrong direction. I'd be willing to make some suggestions and solicit the input of people whose areas of expertise will help set us straight. If you'd like, I'd be happy to form a committee. So, when can we get this rodeo a-runnin'?"

Copy and Paste

The last time my wife, Mary-Jane—a mental health clinician—interviewed for a job, she finished the meeting by plainly stating to her prospective bosses (who were interviewing her as a team), "I'm very interested in this position. Could you tell me where I stand?" They asked her to leave the room. A few minutes later, they brought her back in and said, "You've got it!" Imagine how many people don't enjoy such a rewarding encounter because they never bother to ask outright for the thing they seek.

Similarly, if you're recommending a plan to a group of people, always end with a request to get started. Always come right out and ask for it (just like asking for the job at the end of the job interview). Advertising expert Barry Callen claims that including a "call to action" in an ad increases results by as much as 20 percent!

Add a Rhyme Every Time

Weak: "Please follow our rules for safety."

Powerful: "Safety first, or call the hearse!"

Sometimes a clever catchphrase is important if remembering the information is as important as people remembering you. If your trademark line is such a mnemonic, perfect. Perhaps a rhyme will do the trick. If you say to your barber, "Keep it short, sport," you'll only have to say it once or twice before he remembers you and how you like your hair trimmed.

What should we know about how to treat others? "It's cool to follow the Golden Rule." What should kids know about approaching people they don't know? "It's a danger to talk to a stranger." What is a cop on the day shift most proud of? "Saving lives, home by five." Get it?

Example: "Hey, Roy, you know you're not allowed to work on that circuit box without turning off the juice. Let's get that power shut off and locked out the right way. Safety first, or call the hearse!"

Use an Old Phrase a New Way

Weak: "I work hard to write down all observations."

Powerful: "I walk softly and carry a big marker!"

With a banner in the background that read "Mission Accomplished" on the USS *Abraham Lincoln* in 2003, President George W. Bush gave a speech meant to signal a turning point of the war in Iraq. When it became clear later on that the situation in Iraq was worsening dramatically, the phrase "Mission Accomplished" became something of a joke line to mock any failed endeavor. At this writing, no one dares use the phrase—especially on a banner—to congratulate someone for a job well done for fear of being ridiculed.

Example: "We know you all appreciate this fresh fruit and these pies, or you wouldn't be here today for this festival. But I'm sure you've all read that we've had a pretty tough season on this farm. If you want to see these orchards stick around, please keep patronizing us, and tell your friends to stop by, too. Ask not what your country farmer can do for you. Ask what you can do for your country farmer."

State the Obvious

Weak: "That new employee seems very enthusiastic."

Powerful: "Now *that's* what I call *highly* motivated!"

There's nothing wrong with pointing out the incredibly obvious, especially if you want to make sure that everyone has seen it, and if you want to make sure that everyone has heard *you* in the process. It can be obnoxious if overdone. If not, it's not a bad trademark line. "Now *that's* a great report!" "Now *that's* a well-planned vacation!" And the list goes on.

It's worth mentioning that what's obvious to you isn't always obvious to everyone. I regularly test college students on the main points of short essays they read and are immediately asked to summarize. It's amazing how little people mentally digest. Maybe we're all too saturated with electronic stimuli. And so, if you point out something obvious and you see many heads turn as if it's the first time they're noticing it, don't be surprised. You have found your trademark!

Example: "That new employee showed up an hour early today, read through all the technical manuals, and is now through half the pile of specs we placed on her desk for comment. Now *that's* what I call *highly* motivated."

Highlight and Delete

Watch the cute sayings or catchphrases around bad news. You certainly don't want your trademark tied to poor social judgment or to the news itself. For example, if your work team were being told about a colleague's terminal illness, you wouldn't say, "Well, let's stay chipper, Skipper!"

Use a Simile

Weak: "That seems a bit confusing."

Powerful: "That's as puzzling as a Rubik's Cube with one color!"

A *simile* isn't quite as clever as a metaphor (mentioned in Chapter 1). But it still makes for an interesting trademark line. "That guy's as smooth as a cold beer on a hot summer day." The comparison appeals to people's visceral responses and thus keeps their attention. It's also much more remarkable than saying, "Yeah, he's a smooth talker."

def•i•ni•tion

A **simile** is a figure of speech that compares two things using either *like* or *as*. ("Her voice is like an angel's voice" or "Her voice is as sweet as an angel's.")

A simile is not quite the same as a metaphor, which involves a comparison without *like* or *as*. ("The boss is a grizzly in the morning.")

If you constantly remind someone to "stay as cool as a cucumber," he'll remember the line, and you'll be known as the "cool as a cucumber" versifier.

Example: "Are you the manager? I want to pay you a compliment. I've never seen customer service as cordial as the assistance your new representative gave me. A nice smile, lots of patience, plenty of know-how—and an offer to call me later to make sure everything was working okay. That type of support is as warm as a new puppy on Christmas morning. Keep hiring people like that, and keep up the great work!"

The Least You Need to Know

- A well-crafted trademark line will help people remember you and the things you say in a positive way.

- To form a good catchphrase, try a word or two that's well known but not often used. Keep your catchphrase positive and use it when people could use a lift.

- Use your trademark line to agree with some parts of what others are saying, even if you disagree with other parts.

- Try playing with words, such as repeating the same word, rhyming words, or using similes.

- Ask rhetorical questions when they're appropriate, and ask questions requiring important answers when *they're* appropriate.

- Try using an old catchphrase in a new way, especially a catchphrase with which people are familiar.

Chapter 7

Add Punch to Your Main Points

In This Chapter

- Verbal cues to "listen up!"
- Strong supporting points
- Robust endings
- Applauding the process
- Praising people

Are you presenting your important thoughts verbally, perhaps to your work team, your colleagues, or to a group of bosses? There are some powerful, proven words and phrases that are prone to spice up your declarations.

The following power words help you to introduce your main points, shore them up, brandish them, and bring them home. There are also a few points here regarding talking up people.

Offer Verbal Cues to the Listener

Weak: "It is so, because …"

Powerful: "In fact, …"

To the extent that words are powerful (and they really are), there's nothing more powerful than a good *verbal cue*. If you can instantaneously order another person to "Listen up to this important point," then you've got a useful tool. If people can't concentrate on your great argument, how are you ever going to convince them of anything?

def•i•ni•tion

A **verbal cue** is a word or group of words that signals a transition to the listener. This prompt might be a specific request for an action, or it might be a hint that something different is about to happen or be said.

There's really nothing wrong with the word *because*. However, sometimes, it's a little weak, well, because people expect you to say it when you're making a point. As a result, they tune out.

The phrase "in fact" garners a listener's attention. It's a very powerful verbal light switch that hooks the listener into focusing on your next supporting point.

Example: "I'm here today to offer some fascinating findings from our consumer study. As many of you know, our study suggests that the trend away from plastic shoes has accelerated. In fact, the data indicate that we should reduce production of our plastic, multicolored line by 75 percent for next spring."

Weak: "Unexpectedly …"

Powerful: "Surprisingly …" (or "Astonishingly …")

If you tell your audience that something happened "unexpectedly," it might unintentionally suggest that you don't know what you're doing or that you're not in control. On the other hand, if you tell them that something happened "surprisingly" or, perhaps better still, "astonishingly," then the implication is that any professional would have been caught off guard by the same happening.

Also, the word *surprisingly* has greater potential to turn the attention switch back on if listeners have turned it off.

Example: "As you know, the department recently increased the requirements for a student to score an A on this exam. Surprisingly, the raw scores went down dramatically. Of course, we expected the letter-grade averages to drop because of the higher percentage requirement. But we were frankly astonished that the raw scores dropped. Apparently, when students realized they weren't going to get an "easy" A, many of them gave up on the test altogether."

Weak: "Obviously ..."

Powerful: "Without a doubt ..."

The word *obviously* holds a certain snobbishness that turns people off. When you say *obviously*, people might hear, "What, are you—some kind of idiot?" Should you understand this point? Obviously! Hmmm, a bit condescending.

But when you say "without a doubt," you imply, "Yes, I believe the evidence clearly shows this." And again, it's a nice verbal signal that immediately regains the interest of the inattentive listener.

One small warning: there are always doubts and downsides to every recommendation. If you use the phrase "without a doubt," apply it to the strong supporting point rather than to the overriding recommendation.

Example: "Without a doubt, there are people who are not eligible registering to vote under this new law. After this election is over, we're going to discover that, under its inadequate provisions for enforcement, this law allowed thousands of people in our state to commit voter fraud and to hold unfair influence over the election results."

Make Your Support Stronger

Weak: "Here's how we think it'll work."

Powerful: "Here's how a trial program worked."

There's no success like verified success. And there's no verified success like that effectively conveyed to others. It's one thing to offer a manifesto to other people; it's quite another to say, "Here's how this has worked for other people like you."

If you don't have the time or the resources to set up a trial, look for the results of a trial similar to the one you would have liked to run. It's not a perfect comparison, but it's better than no trial at all.

Example: "In a trial group of 300 people, we found that more than 80 percent of the home-breakfast eaters who sampled this new cereal said they would be inclined to purchase it in the grocery store."

Weak: "For instance ..."

Powerful: "To illustrate this point ..."

Highlight and Delete

Don't tailor, exaggerate, or falsify the results of an experiment meant to back up your claim. Either conduct another trial or fess up. Counterfeit results have ruined many a career.

"For instance" has a spontaneous sound to it, as if you were coming up with an example off the top of your head. It's not a fair interpretation of the phrase, but, unfortunately, that's sometimes the air it gives off. If you're about to tell a story about someone or something that typifies your central theme, call it an illustration and signal that it's about to start.

Offering to illustrate a point sounds strong, knowledgeable, and prepared. Plus, it adds nicely to your arsenal of supporting facts and statistics. An illustration may be one sample, but if it appropriately represents a bigger picture, it does so in a very effective, attention-grabbing way.

Example: "To illustrate this point, I refer you to Lucy, a nurse at your hospital who dramatically increased her computer proficiency by attending one of our training programs."

Weak: "Also ..."

Powerful: "Furthermore ..."

Similar to the instance/illustration contrast, "also" has the weakening impact of sounding like you're adding points at the last minute to shore up a feeble case. "Furthermore," on the other hand, implies that there's so much more to say about your contention that you can't help but add one more dramatic point.

Furthermore, the word *furthermore* cues the listener to pay attention, because more supporting evidence is forthcoming. Many times, the goal of a power word is not simply to intensify what you have to say but to draw attention, when it matters, to the points you're making.

Example: "Furthermore, Patricia has demonstrated her ability to handle very tough cases with little notice, and to bring about much the same result as other employees do with much more preparation and assistance."

Offer Other Key Supporting Phrases

Weak: "Meets our requirements."

Powerful: "Meets our high standards."

Along with offering that a plan is strategically sound and perceptive, there are some other ways to talk up a new set of procedures.

Don't say that a new course of action meets some type of mandatory requirement. That's bad for two reasons: 1) it implies that the only reason for doing it is that you're being forced to (making you sound reactive instead of proactive), and 2) it sounds as if you're taking steps to fulfill some minimum requisite, as opposed to doing something spectacular that sets your organization apart.

Brag that new action brings your team up to a level of professionalism you've always expected but are only now beginning proudly to attain.

Example: "These new disclosure regulations meet the high standards we set for ourselves some time ago. We're proud to offer them as a standard for other businesses in the public eye to follow."

Weak: "Fulfills our obligations."

Powerful: "Honors the promises we have made."

Again, don't offer something as if it were being done so begrudgingly. Maybe it is, but if you have to do it anyway, and if it took lots of time and sweat, you might as well put a positive, boastful spin on it.

Place your recent actions in the context of a special public commitment or a vow of caring for your customers or your team members. Offer it as something that fits in with *many* things you do, in similar fashion, to set yourself apart from others in a superior way. Say, "This particular action continues to make us the special team that we've always been."

Example: "Reopening this murder case honors the promises we have made to this community. It's not simply a matter of succumbing to public opinion: it's a matter of winning back a public trust that has been lost."

Weak: "Appropriate."

Powerful: "Timely."

You want to make sure, when announcing something new, that you sound like the dog wagging its tail—and not the dog being wagged by its tail. That is, you want to sound as if you're controlling the system and not the other way around.

The word *appropriate* sounds reactive, as if you wouldn't be doing something if people or circumstances weren't forcing you to do so. The word *timely*, on the other hand, sounds as if you're on the ball and you're making the right things happen at the right time.

Example: "And so, in light of this prevalent, in-your-face corruption, it's timely that we end the practice of allowing nonelected officials to decide who receives state grant money and who doesn't."

Talk Up the Process

Weak: "A legal process."

Powerful: "An open and ethical process."

Be a cheerleader for an ongoing plan, especially one that you're in charge of. Reminding people why this plan is important makes them feel good to be a part of it, and it makes them feel good about having you around!

Although many programs go through rigorous legal scrutiny, and although that scrutiny takes lots of time and energy, you might not want to brag about enduring it. Saying a process is "legal" is rather weak on the gusto-meter.

Instead, appeal to your audience's sense of righteousness by touting a plan's openness and moral rectitude. People want more than legality: they want to know what's going on.

Example: "The point of this open and ethical process is to ensure that public employers are not secretly creating jobs and then placing their family members and the family members of their cronies in those jobs."

Weak: "Imaginative."

Powerful: "Creative and method-enhancing."

The word *imaginative* suggests that the team behind the process have their heads in the clouds. The word (unfairly) evokes a child sitting at his school desk, staring at the ceiling while more important things are taking place at the front of the classroom.

Maximizing Maxim

My colleague Steven Baron, known for his verbal vigor, suggests that the nodding of heads is the best sign that you're onto something. "If you're praising a plan, and you see heads nodding, continue its praise. If the heads aren't nodding, best to move on to another bullet point!"

If you want to express approval for a team's or process's creativity, then refer specifically to that part of the creativity that adds to the organization. For example, if someone's ingenuity streamlines a process, then address the new efficiency along with the ingenuity.

Example: "This plan for increasing our web security is creative and method-enhancing to the point where we're ahead of anyone who might hack into our system and, at the same time, we're making the set-up easier for any of our employees."

Weak: "Moving."

Powerful: "Inspiring."

Suggesting that something stirs emotions does not necessarily mean that it's getting anything accomplished. The novel and movie *Love Story* was moving, but author Erich Segal didn't do my taxes for me—see what I'm saying?

"Inspiring," however, involves more than emotion. Yes, emotions come into play, but there are tangible results attached to those emotions. An inspiring plan or institution makes people feel good about themselves and about being a part of the big picture. As a result, they tend to produce desired outcomes, many times without being urged or overly prodded.

Example: "This plan for offering a college education to poor children is inspiring. It finds those 'diamonds in the rough' that will benefit most. It funds them in an economical manner. And, most important, it allows society to benefit from a truly smart person who otherwise might have been idle."

Talk Up the People

Weak: "Headstrong and daring."

Powerful: "Assertive and courageous."

People like to hear their own names. They also appreciate nice things being said about them, especially in front of their families and/or colleagues.

However, many times a word can have two meanings, with the second meaning working as a discourteous undercurrent, either intentionally or unintentionally. Words such as *headstrong* and *daring* might be taken to mean "pigheaded" and "foolhardy."

Try to use words that carry as few second meanings as possible. *Assertive* is one such word. *Courageous* is another.

Example: "I can't say enough good things about Andrew. His leadership in this area of reform has been assertive and courageous. His changes, though not easy to push through, have benefited this department and this company."

Weak: "Kind."

Powerful: "Selfless."

There's something about the word *kind* that implies that someone is a pushover. "He's a kind soul." You know—the kind of person who gives a handout to the guy with one hand extended while the other hand holds a bottle of Mad Dog 20/20, all the while promising not to spend the money on alcohol.

Try a word that'll hold a bit more backbone. I recommend *selfless*. A selfless person is caring and mentoring and bighearted, but there's a tone to the word suggesting that he's also dignified and just in administering his consideration. *Selfless* may also be used in ways that have little to do with charity. A selfless boss, for example, might be a staunch disciplinarian but eager to teach and to serve the team.

Example: "Ken is one of those selfless people this organization needs more of. There are no ulterior motives behind Ken's good deeds. He helps others for the sake of helping, and he draws satisfaction from watching others succeed."

Weak: "Capable." (or "Proficient.")

Powerful: "Competent." (or "Skilled.")

Some words such as *capable* or *proficient* imply a person meets the minimum requirements for a particular job or task.

Maximizing Maxim

My boss Bill Krug, a teacher and teaching administrator for 30 years, suggests that complimenting someone in public garners the best results when it doesn't generate jealousy or resentment. "The other people in the room shouldn't feel diminished by your flattering remarks toward that one person," he says. "Instead, they should feel good about that person's being noticed, and they should feel that, next time around, it could be any one of them getting the praise."

If you want to pay someone a compliment regarding her job skills, use words that suggest her work aptitude goes above and beyond what is expected of anyone in the same title.

Example: "Jen is highly competent, especially in those areas where such competence is hard to find. When the computers throughout this company shut down and everyone else is twiddling his or her thumbs, Jen is shining a flashlight on the old, trustworthy engineering tables, calculating the numbers by hand."

End on a Robust Note

Weak: "So once again ..."

Powerful: "As I have pointed out ..."

I passionately subscribe to the old Dale Carnegie notion that you should tell people what you're about to tell them, then tell it to them, and then tell them what you just told them. And so, I wholeheartedly recommend that you recap your main points at the end of any presentation.

> **Copy and Paste**
>
> Whenever possible, end your presentation by relating your main points back to a need the organization has. If your suggestions fit a specific and recognizable deficiency, they're most likely to get the attention of others.

Of course, you could always say, "In conclusion." That's sure to wake up those in the crowd who were daydreaming or outright sleeping! Maybe a better verbal cue to wrap things up is, "As I have pointed out." It lets people know that you're about to restate the meat of your argument, and it implies that you have done a wonderful job of making your cases up to that point.

Example: "As I have pointed out, the restructuring of this company—painful as it might be initially—will not only make us less vulnerable to hostile market conditions, but will also set us up to be much more competitive once the crisis is over."

Weak: "Then ..." (or "Therefore ...")

Powerful: "Consequently ..." (or "As a result ...")

The words *then* or *therefore* sometimes seem forced, as if the speaker were trying to impose a connection between a cause and effect that might or might not really be there.

The words *consequently* or *as a result* do a much better job of suggesting an evident correlation. They also suggest a result that the speaker or the audience might not necessarily have wanted but are now obligated to deal with. "Hey, this isn't the outcome I was hoping for," you imply, "but it seems to be the one we're going to have to tackle."

Example: "Consequently, the need to improve our weather station is not a matter of expedience but a matter of survival. Without these equipment augmentations, it is very likely that, within the next five years, our town will be destroyed by another unforeseen, deadly storm."

Weak: "We need to think ahead."

Powerful: "We must continue to be strategic in our thinking."

Don't ever suggest that it's time to start planning for the future. You should have been doing that all along! Even if what you're talking about is one specific, new issue, you don't want to imply that it should have been foreseen but wasn't.

Instead, insinuate that your new strategy for long-term planning is just more of the same, good thinking. After all, we're always looking to the future. But announcing a new strategy for doing so should impress your audience and put them at ease—not make them nervous about the organization's near-sightedness.

Example: "We must continue to be strategic in our thinking. The electric car will help the American family and the American manufacturer that produces it. And, on a grand scale, it will help free us from oil and all the economic shackles that go with it. And, finally, it will help a world looking for less pollution and lower carbon emissions."

The Least You Need to Know

- Verbal cues tell listeners that something important is coming up. Assuming that they won't be concentrating on everything you say, verbal cues signal to listeners when to focus on your main ideas.

- Use proven success stories, illustrations, and tangible evidence whenever possible to support your argument.

- Introduce a new plan or policy as if it falls in line with your organization's traditional values and goals.

- Compliment a process's originality and new insights in ways that still draw attention to its tangible benefits and accomplishments.

◆ Flatter people in ways that not only praise their personal attributes but also address how these qualities make concrete differ-
ences for the team. Avoid complimentary words that carry second
meanings.

◆ Always end on a strong, passionate note.

Chapter 8

Use Charisma to Make People Feel Good

In This Chapter

- ◆ Prompting people to like you and to like themselves
- ◆ Portraying confidence in others
- ◆ Making people feel valued
- ◆ Fostering team unity
- ◆ Offering nonempty compliments and gratitude

When people speak of someone's charisma, you might think they're talking about his nice suit, slick smile, and ability to make people swoon. If that's what they mean, or if that's what you think, then someone is using the word mistakenly. Charisma is essentially your ability to make people like you and, at the same time, to make them like and feel good about themselves. Sure, there's a magnetism that might, at times, go along with the clothing and good looks. But there are ways, without spending money at the tailor, of prompting people to follow you.

Words don't cost a nickel, but if you use them properly, they are powerful affirmations that give you personal appeal.

Remember That Everything's in a Name

Weak: "Good morning."

Powerful: "Good morning, Andy." (With a smile.)

In Chapter 3, I mentioned that a handwritten, mailed thank-you note holds 10 times more impact than a thank-you e-mail or text message. Hey, sometimes the wrapping is more important than the present.

I suggest the same holds true when speaking. Instead of mumbling a "good morning" to someone, wear a smile, speak clearly and confidently, and use the person's name. In fact, remember as many people's names as you can. A person's name is the most important word he hears every day. And most people don't hear their own names enough.

The converse is true as well: over the years, the people I have considered the most miserable and personably dislikable were those who didn't smile or who looked the other way when I said hello. Maybe they were perfectly fine human beings who preferred to keep to themselves. But they held little positive sway over me or anyone else.

Example: (Smiling.) "Good morning, Andy. Beautiful day!"

Tell 'Em You Got Faith

Weak: "Get it done."

Powerful: "I have faith in your ability, and I know you'll make this happen."

I have been yelled at—I mean, uh, redirected—by many a boss over the years. Most times I had it coming. But even so, most times I also left the encounter upset, my bruised ego hurting, and my defense mechanisms smoking after being fully engaged.

There are, however, those times when I left feeling a little less bruised and a lot more encouraged. Those are the times the boss ended by saying that she had overriding faith in my abilities and my professionalism.

What a nice way to end any sort of talk, whether it's disciplinary, motivational, or otherwise. Tell someone that you have faith in her and that you know, when all is said and done, that she will come through for you.

Example: "Patti, I have watched you balance those books at the last minute, flawlessly, a hundred times before. Stop stressing. We all have faith in your ability, and we're all absolutely confident that you're going to make this happen."

Tell 'Em You Need 'Em

Weak: "Get it done."

Powerful: "I'm counting on you."

Instead of begging, nagging, or ordering someone to do something, why not instead tell him that you need him? People like to be needed, and they enjoy feeling appreciated. When someone says "I need you," or "I'm counting on you," the implication is that you have something, no matter how seemingly minor, that few others can readily provide. It creates a wonderful feeling of self-worth.

If you're counting on someone to make something happen, don't downplay your sole dependence on him. Tell him his services are unique. (Of course, if he's got you over a barrel, you had better find someone else with a similar skill.) His feeling of merit is likely to prompt him to get the job done.

> **Maximizing Maxim**
>
> It's nice to be valued, and powerful people respect that notion. Robert McNamara, U.S. Defense Secretary during the Vietnam War, once said, "Brains, like hearts, go where they are appreciated."

Example: "No one does masonry like you do, Kenny. If it's doable for you, I could use this new walkway by tomorrow. I'm counting on you."

Invite Someone to Join You

Weak: "Here's why you need to do what I tell you."

Powerful: "Join me, and let's make this happen."

Sometimes a challenge or a task is best portrayed as a journey. And so, when you ask for someone's help, what you're really asking her for is a partner on the journey. Sound idealistic? It is, and that's why it works.

Instead of telling someone why she needs to get this or that done, invite her on a grand journey with astonishing things along the way and a breathtaking view as well. So you're only painting the living room? Okay, so it's not that romantic. But you tried!

Example: "Join me, and let's make this happen. Let's begin our grand journey toward more honest and more accountable local government in New Jersey."

Mention the Responsibility, Not the Difficulty

Weak: "You'll have to accomplish this menial task before I trust you with more difficult ones."

Powerful: "This is too important a responsibility for just anyone."

Along the lines of telling someone that you're counting on him, as mentioned previously, emphasize the importance of a responsibility—every time—over the amount or level of difficulty involved.

Yes, maybe your child wants to bake using the oven before he knows how to boil water. But if you're prepping dinner together, don't say, "Hey, you gotta learn to boil water before you turn that oven on." Instead, stress the necessity of the boiled water for the entire meal, and make that task important. Eventually he'll understand the small cooking tasks and move up to the more involved ones. And then he'll become a young adult and you'll never see him in the kitchen again.

Highlight and Delete

Don't ever promise someone more work if he accomplishes what he has already done, even if you consider the extra responsibility something of a reward or precursor to promotion. Even the most diligent person will slow things down if he feels he's about to be dumped on.

Example: "Luke, I need you on nights for the convalescent duty. This is too important a responsibility for just anyone. I've seen how well you handle the task of being on your own at night, and I believe the night nurses like having you around."

Respect the Opinion

Weak: "Excuse me while I get an expert opinion."

Powerful: "May I ask your opinion?"

Don't simply recognize the unique skills that people bring to the table (although it's important that you do recognize them). Recognize those things that they bring to the table same as everyone else, but maybe from a different perspective. People generally are a lot smarter than you think they are, and all kinds of people in the workplace notice all kinds of things that you might be missing.

Ask an accountant about the type of copier you're thinking of purchasing. Ask a cab driver about politics. Ask the person who answers the phones about the lighting in the office. You'll be surprised to find important, useful information from all of them. And you'll be one step ahead by holding a different perspective or a counterintuitive point of view.

Example: "Patti, may I ask your opinion? That test alarm goes off every day at 1:30 P.M., just when things are getting started after lunch. What do you think about having it tested at lunch time, when most people won't be bothered by it?"

Use "Would" Instead of "Can"

Weak: "Can you help me?"

Powerful: "Would you please help me?"

According to relationship expert John Gray (who wrote the series of *Men Are from Mars, Women Are from Venus* books), men don't like to be asked, "Can you help me?" Gray argues that a man innately and subliminally thinks that he's simply being asked about his abilities and not for a favor—and no matter how many times a woman might keep asking or dropping a hint, it doesn't fully register with the man!

I suppose we could talk for hours about whether or not men and women are mentally wired differently by nature, but for now, it's worth mentioning that I believe there's something to what Gray is saying.

Don't ask either a man or a woman *can you?*; ask *would you?* instead. And throw a *please* in there to boot. Whether or not it has to do with our mental networking doesn't really matter. If *would you?* gets more results than does *can you?* (and I argue that it does), and if *would you?* sounds more polite than *can you?* (and I argue that it does), then say *would you?* when asking for something. It's effortless, and it carries more impact.

Example: "Excuse me, Kenny. Would you please help me? I need someone to attend tomorrow's staff meeting in my place, and you know the most about the refurbishing project. Would you, please?"

Note the Effort

Weak: "Good job."

Powerful: "Well done!"

More powerful: "It looks like you put a lot of effort into that project."

The phrase "good job," while appreciated, seems a bit clichéd these days—empty, like the phrase "how y'doing?" or "have a nice day."

I suggest that the phrase "well done" is fresh enough to carry a more powerful impact. A complete sentence, with a verb and subject, carries even further. "Hey, you put a lot of hard work into that assignment. Way to go!"

Highlight and Delete _____

> Don't ever think, "Hey, he knows I appreciate him. I don't have to say thanks every time he does some small thing." Oh, yes you do, whether it's a friend, lover, co-worker, or team member. Say thanks loudly and often. And say it from the heart. It registers psychologically in ways we still don't fully understand. (Oh, and for the lover, say, "I love you," just as much. He or she needs to hear that, too.)

Example: "I couldn't believe what I saw when I walked into the room, Andy. That's very professional craftsmanship. It looks like you put a lot of effort into that project. Thanks so much. We're lucky to have you around here."

Offer Thanks and Then Thanks Again

Weak: "Thanks."

Powerful: "Thanks, Jim. I appreciate your time." (And maybe a quick, handwritten thank-you note to back it up.)

When you offer thanks, offer it from the heart. Look the person in the eye. Thank him for his time and energy. Use his first name. The more you convey your gratitude, the more likely he'll work hard for you the next time around.

And again, I can't say enough about a handwritten thank-you note, sent via the U.S. Postal Service or via interoffice mail. (If your interoffice mail is slower than snail mail—and I have worked at such places—admit as much and pop the note with a stamp in the box at the local post office.)

Example: "Jim, thanks so much for stopping by and offering your expertise. I appreciate your time, and you saved us a couple of hours of ours. May the team treat you to lunch sometime this week?"

The Least You Need to Know

- Say things that prompt people to think good things about you and about themselves. Say good things that make people remember you.

- Tell people that you respect their skills, that you trust them with tasks, and that you're counting on them to make big things happen.

- Say things that make people feel valued and wanted.

- Constantly offer compliments and words of gratitude. Follow up your verbal thanks with written thank-you notes.

Part 3

Power Words as Responses

Just as a martial arts expert draws strength from countering his or her opponents' moves, the power-word specialist acquires control by responding to others in commanding ways.

The purpose of using power words isn't to dominate others or to one-up people. Rather, the intention of these words and phrases is to get others to act in ways that benefit you. There's no better way to channel people in your preferred direction than to lower their defenses, display to them a level of understanding, and set up positive communication on your terms.

The power phrase, as a response, is like a boomerang with a wicked arc; it catches the thrower off guard. Such responses include disarming phrases, empathetic phrases, and phrases that change the course of the conversation.

9

Disarm Your Opponents

In This Chapter

- ◆ Lowering your opponent's barriers
- ◆ Putting your adversary at ease
- ◆ Starting from a point of cooperation
- ◆ The value of respecting opposing opinion
- ◆ Finding common ground

Mankind, unfortunately, seems to learn and relearn throughout the centuries that war doesn't mean completely conquering an adversary. What's the point of controlling an annihilated territory? Gaining real power doesn't mean wiping out your enemy; it means getting your enemy to behave in a manner that is to your benefit.

The first step in pointing your enemy in a preferred direction of behavior is to lower his or her defenses. Disarm your opponents through words and actions. Lay the foundation for productive dialogue. Then build a bridge from that initial, opposing viewpoint to your way of thinking.

Suggest That You're Amenable and Amendable

Weak: "You're wrong."

Powerful: "Perhaps you're right."

Which is stronger—a doll made of plastic or a doll made of rubber? Yes, the plastic doll seems more rigid and durable, at least until it's tossed across the room and an arm snaps off. The flexible, pliable rubber doll is stretched, stomped on, and put through all sorts of tests—but it bends with the pressure and stays around for a long time.

The same notion, I suggest, pertains to dealing with people. Over the years, I have watched my own stubbornness and the stubbornness of others create huge setbacks. Conversely, I have learned and utilized the benefits of flexibility. No one wants to be known as a pushover, but in reality, nothing really happens in the way of new ideas and new agreements until someone in the room bends a bit. Go ahead and bend.

> **Copy and Paste**
>
> When you listen to an opposing opinion, do it for more than just courtesy. By opening your mind, you'll often discover, within that opinion, something of value.

Quite often, as soon as you mention the possibility of your being wrong, the other person will concede the point anyway. He wasn't looking to take his bad idea to the grave: he was simply trying to save face, whether it was in the break room with just you or in a conference room packed with colleagues. And if he doesn't bend a little (as you are bending) at that moment, he might do so later.

Example: "Perhaps you're right. Maybe I should go with a more traditional method for staffing that position. I'd like to hear more about your earlier thoughts on the subject. When can we sit down and talk about it?"

Don't Give Someone the Shine

Weak: "I'll look into it."

Powerful: "You're right—there *is* room for improvement."

When you say to someone, "I'll look into it," you might as well be telling her, "I'll forget about it as soon as I walk away." And for good reason: if you're an important and busy person, it's likely (and perfectly reasonable) that you *will* forget it. That's why she's bringing it up to you—because you're important and busy. But in contradiction, that's also why you're going to forget.

Instead of disrespecting (and further upsetting) someone by immediately disregarding what she's suggesting, why not offer that person the courtesy of paying attention and jotting down her concern in your daytime planner (or electronic organizer)? Then, at the very least, she knows you're going to see it and consider it again. It's an easy, professional way to disarm an adverse team member.

Example: "You're right—there is room for improvement. In fact, you make a great point: if this hospital were to streamline its billing the way you describe, we'd save a lot of money. Let me jot it down right now, and I'll mention it to our Accounts Receivable folks as soon as possible."

Give Up the Toffee to Get the Bon-Bon

Weak: "All of your views are wrong, especially the one regarding Item Z (the most important item to you)."

Powerful: "I tend to agree with your views regarding Items X and Y, and I like your reasoning behind those views. Would you mind if we take another look at Item Z?"

Disarming your adversary doesn't mean conceding something that you find important—it means conceding something *he* finds important. Therefore, you should place a polite value on those points you are willing to forfeit: you might wind up giving up something he cares passionately about but that you (privately) don't really care about one way or the other.

> **Maximizing Maxim**
>
> The art of creating a good deal for everyone is very much a gift. As *Forbes* magazine founder B. F. Forbes once noted, "The bargain that yields mutual satisfaction is the only one that is apt to be repeated."

There's no rule that says that, to display power, you need to begin from the point of confrontation and stubbornness and then back into a position of negotiation. When you begin a process by seeking the middle ground, you do it from strength by being the one to set the initial terms for the cooperation. In doing so, you manage to hide your sense of what items are important.

Once again, negotiation is not a sign of weakness. The wealthiest, most powerful people in the world got that way because of their ability to bargain.

Example: "I tend to agree with your thoughts on purchasing the restaurant and the miniature golf course, and I like your reasoning behind those views. Would you mind if we take another look at our company's possible, additional purchase of the penny arcade?"

Let 'Em Vent

Weak: "I disagree with that."

Powerful: "What do *you* suggest?"

It sometimes pays to cut right to the chase. If someone is complaining to you or resisting an idea of yours, don't fight over it. Instead, ask the person right away what solution he seeks.

Often, a person is simply looking to vent his feelings or his misgivings, not to quarrel. By eliciting a suggestion from him, you recognize his initial misgivings and help to get (or keep) him on your side. When you ask a person "What do you suggest?" you'll often hear a response along the lines of: "Well, I guess I don't have a better idea—I'm just worried about how this new plan is going to affect my department." Hear him out. Let him vent. He might wind up being your most ardent supporter because you allowed him the courtesy of mulling over his uncertainties.

Example: "From what you're saying, it seems you're having trouble with this new plan. What do *you* suggest?"

Don't Demean

Weak: "You can't be serious."

Powerful: "Your idea has a lot of potential, but I'm wondering about the time involved. Is there some way that we could make the process shorter?"

By this point in the book, I've undoubtedly let down the occasional sociopath who purchased it. Power words aren't about putting down other people or belittling their ideas. I'm sure there's a book out there about one-upmanship. This book isn't it. True power is about getting things done without hindrance from others. It's not really about towering over others.

Even the dumbest idea has some merit to it. Instead of putting someone in conflict mode by questioning the seriousness of her idea, compliment the good intention behind the idea and, perhaps, some part of the idea that's not too outlandish. Then, ask the person to address your specific, larger concern. Sometimes, she'll instantly recognize the folly of her idea. Other times, she might still be convinced about the soundness of her own idea. Still other times, you might change your mind and recognize a worthy, if unconventional, idea. In any case, you're likely to have made an advocate instead of an enemy.

 Highlight and Delete

Don't offer someone the floor (i.e., attention from others in the room) to catch the person off guard and humiliate her. People are more likely to remember your nastiness than whatever topic was being discussed. And you'll have an enemy for a very long time.

Example: "Your idea regarding screen doors on our submarine has a lot of potential, but I'm wondering how the water will stay out. Is there some way that we could reap the benefits of ventilation but, at the same time, ensure a safe water lock?"

Suggest That They Didn't Really Mean It

Weak: "How dare you say such a thing!"

Powerful: "I'm sure you didn't mean to imply she was unreliable when you said ... but that's how she took it."

Not everything in this book can be used when addressing a boss, but this particular power phrase seems to work pretty well with both underlings and superiors. This phrase falls along the lines of: "Uh, boss, is that what you *really* mean to say?" If the boss says, "You're darned right," well, then, you have your marching orders (or your harsh statement). If the boss gets that you're trying to help him out by keeping him in check, then he might say something like, "You have a point—let me retract that one." If what he said was impertinent, he may offer an apology on the spot.

Even at West Point, where students are stringently held to their words, a cadet is allowed immediately to withdraw a "pop off" answer. Sometimes, all people need is to have the answer politely pointed out and to have the space and opportunity to make it right.

Example: "I'm sure you didn't mean to imply that the maid was filthy and uncaring when you said that her rag looked too old and dirty, but I thought you should know that that's how she took it. She seems pretty down from the remark."

> ### Maximizing Maxim
>
> In his masterful text *Leadership in Organizations* (Prentice Hall, 2006), Gary Yukl proposes that it is possible to have an impact not only on your peers and your assistants but also on your superiors. Saying the right things, offering advice, and showing that you care for the team is often accepted and appreciated by managers.
>
> Yukl calls this notion coaching the boss. "Subordinates ... have opportunities to coach the boss, especially one who is new and inexperienced."

Disarm Them with Confidence

Weak: "I think I can."

Powerful: "No problem."

I'm all for setting expectations relatively low and then dazzling people with my ability to exceed those expectations. I dare say I've made a career out of it! My mom and my wife can see through my scheme, but not too many others.

On the other hand, sometimes setting expectations high has its tactical worth. There are many people in our lives who like to watch an insecure person squirm under pressure. It makes for a wonderful, sadistic pastime. And it makes them (wrongly) feel better about themselves. If you bump into this kind of person, defuse her game and shut her down with your over-the-top confidence. "You need it tomorrow? No problem." "There's no one around to give me a hand? No problem." "The big boss wants to grill me on how I'm going to get it done? No problem." Eventually, the game will stop, and people will become impressed by you (even if they don't want to admit it).

It's worth noting that a good dose of integrity needs to be mixed in with your confidence. Don't say you are able to do something if you're not. But if you're technically proficient and the only thing standing in the way of you and task completion is a little bit of enthusiasm and confidence, then say, "No problem," and impress the heck out of the other people with your self-assurance and your work ethic.

Example: "No problem. I think I can have this sidewalk dug up, hauled out, and replaced by the end of the week. Which new pattern out of the catalog do you like?"

Imply That the Ground Is Common

Weak: "We're on different sides of this issue."

Powerful: "We're saying the same thing, but from different vantage points."

If you and someone else are diametrically opposite on an issue, you don't have to admit it. Suggesting that there's more common ground than perhaps there really is serves as a nice way to disarm an opponent and to get him a little closer to your side. Plus, it fosters a future commonality that's good for all involved. This sense of shared aims and team spirit doesn't mean that everyone will agree on all things, but it does mean that people generally feel good about the team's common mission and overreaching philosophy.

Saying something such as, "We're closer on this issue than you think we are," is a great way to bring down someone's defenses. His first (spoken or unspoken) response will be: "Umm, we are?" And you can explain to him why there's more common ground than he thinks there is.

If you can't find *anything* common, point out that you're both passionate on the same issue. Let the fact that you're arguing about it be your commonality. "Well, one thing is for sure: we both love this topic, and we both love to debate it."

Example: "As I see it, we're saying the same thing, but from different vantage points. We both agree that it's time for a new car. We both agree on the amount that we're willing to spend. Now, it's just a matter of agreeing on the make, model, and color."

If the Ground Isn't Common, Find Some

Weak: "Let's further discuss this topic we disagree upon."

Powerful: "Hey, how about those Jets?"

This phrase isn't about changing the subject. Okay, maybe it is. Alright, I admit it: it's absolutely about changing the subject. Let's face it—sometimes it's best to diffuse the hostility by temporarily moving on to another topic. Don't ignore the person: that might make her angrier. Simply ask for some cool-off time. Let a different conversation on a different subject be the common ground that starts positive conversation on the initial topic.

Need some common-ground topics? Well, there's the weather. There are activities: "Seen any good movies lately?" There are the topics of kids or vacation plans. There are also restaurants or shopping places. Sound like small talk? It is.

Avoid gossip and mutual complaining. Avoid the saddest items in the news.

Copy and Paste _____

Remember that belongingness is an inherent, human need. People like to belong to groups, they like to be accepted by those groups, and they often are dedicated to the precepts of those groups. If evoking the passionate motto or principles of a group you both belong to sets a collective tone for your two-way discussion, by all means use (but don't abuse) your membership as common ground.

The good thing about small talk is that it often leads to big talk—er, pleasant and productive talk. Eventually, you'll get back to the tough topic that was causing a stir.

Example: "Well, let's cool off for a little bit and get back to this tough topic later. Did you happen to see the rainbow outside our building this morning? It was beautiful."

Seek Actual, If Not Figurative, Common Ground

Weak: "Let's talk about it in my office." (or "… in your office.")

Powerful: "Let's talk about it at the coffee shop."

Although this book doesn't concentrate on meetings or body language (I've written other books on those topics), it's important to mention in this chapter that a good way to disarm your opponent is to find a neutral, physical territory to discuss an issue. Sometimes, seeking actual common ground is as vital as finding figurative common ground.

The movie *The Illusionist* has an interesting scene in which people visiting the sinister Crown Prince Leopold must travel down a hallway packed with hundreds of mounted moose antlers. The implication is clear: I am a grand hunter, and if you cross me, I will kill you. Although not quite so imposing, we all have similar "I love me" stuff on the walls of our offices. At the military school where I teach during the day, some of the officers have very impressive plaques and awards and combat photos. Presumably, the décor of these offices is meant to intimidate new cadet candidates. I'm guessing it works!

If you feel that the surroundings of your office or the office of another will intrude upon a conversation, seek neutral turf to discuss the topic.

Example: "It's a bit stuffy in this building today. There's a great coffee shop down the street that just opened, and it's a beautiful day. How about we continue this conversation over a cup of java?"

The Least You Need to Know

◆ Generally speaking, little happens in this world until someone gives in a bit. If you're interested in wonderful new ideas and new plans, you're going to have to negotiate.

◆ When you differ with someone, immediately seek the middle ground. By doing so, you set the initial terms of negotiation, which helps you disguise the things you *really* seek in the compromise.

◆ Allow your opponent to vent. Even if he gets very little in the process, he might eventually be one of your strongest supporters because you showed him respect by allowing him to speak his piece.

◆ If you hear something that is outrageous or offensive (even from a boss), allow the person to retract it by privately asking, "Is that really what you meant to say?"

◆ Displaying confidence—especially confidence that you can back up—is a quick, easy way to neutralize or win over a detractor.

◆ Common ground is a great weapon; it may be figurative (a common interest for discussion) or actual (a coffee shop where ideas may be discussed without distraction).

10

Mirror People's Thoughts

In This Chapter

- ◆ Mirroring and its origins
- ◆ Using statements to gather info
- ◆ Using powerful, open-ended questions
- ◆ Letting people talk
- ◆ Getting people to own up

Do you want to impress a first date? Do you want to dazzle a prospective boss on a job interview? Do you want to make your spouse love you more or make your kids appreciate you more? Here's a great way to do it: apply effective listening skills and make sure the other person does at least twice as much talking as you do, if not more.

The problem with listening skills these days isn't that people choose not to listen or that they're too busy to listen. I respectfully suggest that, over a generation or two, people have simply lost their proficiency at listening. That is, no one really knows *how* to listen effectively anymore.

I refer you, then, to the great master of listening skills—the pioneering psychologist Carl Rogers. In the 1950s, Rogers became famous advocating a tactic used in active listening that eventually became known as *mirroring*. The goal of these Rogerian phrases is to let people know you're interested, to get them to reflect on what it is they're saying, and to put them on your side.

Reflect What You Hear

Weak: "What's wrong?" (Responding to "I'm not having a good day.")

Powerful: "So your day's not going well."

Many times, the best way to prompt someone to elaborate is to repeat, slightly reworded, what the person has just said. "I'm having a tough time studying." "So your exam prep's not going well." "I'm having a tough time with my kid." "So your child's giving you trouble." It's amazing how much a person opens up when he hears a version of what he has just said thrown back at him. It makes him talk more; it allows him to ponder what he has just said and how he, himself, might make things right. And it gives you a friend for life because you've shown yourself to be a caring, active listener.

def•i•ni•tion

> **Mirroring** is a tactic used by very effective listeners, such as professional counselors, in which the listener "mirrors" certain phrases or paraphrases back to the person talking in order to encourage the person to talk and to reveal more about himself. Mirroring is part of the counseling philosophy established by renowned psychologist Carl Rogers—what he called "the reflection of attitudes."

Of course, not all of this is touchy-feely stuff. Being in a position of power means having access to current and useful information. Power is more than projecting information outward; it also entails gathering data in ways that don't intimidate and that elicit accurate details. You can't make good decisions if you don't really know what's going on.

Example: (After someone says, "I'm worried about the bullies in my neighborhood.") "So some cruel kids in your neighborhood are making you concerned."

Don't Make It *All* About You

Weak: "I know exactly what you mean. It reminds me of the time I once …"

Powerful: "Hmmm …"

They say that the things we hate the most about others are those things that we dislike about ourselves. If that's so, then I must have a bad habit of relating items in a conversation back to my own life situation— because I sure hate it when other people do it to me. "I just bought a new car." "Ahhh, that reminds me of *my* last auto purchase." "I haven't been feeling well." "Oh, let me tell you about *my* last illness." Hey, it's not *all* about you. So why do you keep interrupting with your own life story?

A good conversation involves a lot of give and take. If you're truly a superb conversationalist, you're taking in a lot more than what you're giving out. In other words, you're listening a lot more than you're talking. People love and respect a skilled listener, especially because such a person is so rare these days.

Instead of immediately responding to someone's comment with a story about yourself, say, "Hmmm," showing the person that you're interested, and let the science of great listening begin.

Example: (After someone says, "I'm worried that our company isn't following the same ethical code that it did when we first began working here.") "Hmmm." (And if the person doesn't continue, you use the mirroring technique mentioned earlier in the chapter.)

Throw It Back Differently

Weak: "Let me repeat what you just said."

Powerful: "So people were giving you a rough time today."

The process of mirroring is enhanced when you say something back to someone slightly different from how you just heard it. Of course, there's nothing wrong with repeating what you've just heard verbatim: that's a nice, basic way of letting someone know that you're listening. But when you restate what you've heard in your *own* words, and the person hears it just a little changed from how she said it, it not only tells her that you're in tune and trying to understand, but it also encourages her to elaborate.

Copy and Paste

Lean forward when you listen. Don't fold your arms. If it's possible to conduct the conversation without a table or desk between you, do so. If the person is making heartfelt recommendations, jot them down briefly, as if to follow up on them later. These few small things will make the person open up. You'll gain lots of information (if that's what you seek) and the person's friendship (if that's what you seek).

Paraphrase what you've just heard. Don't change the meaning or add words. Take the same number of words, if not fewer, to say it back in a different way. Doing so will push the person to open up. And it will reveal you as a champion listener, a good friend, and someone very much in sync with the people around you.

Example: (After someone says, "I couldn't get anything started today because people wouldn't stop walking in and interrupting me.") "So folks kept disrupting your work today."

Use a Statement Instead of a Question

Weak: "What's eatin' you?"

Powerful: "Sounds like you're upset."

Someone in your midst is in a horrible mood, and he's grumbling at just about everything. Option Number One is probably to leave the immediate area. But suppose that you have to work or live with this person. Or suppose that you're in charge of or responsible for that person. What should you say? "Holy cow! Who spit in your cereal this morning?" Nah, that won't work.

Many times, the person is unaware that he's giving off upset vibes. Drawing attention to these vibes in a negative way is likely to make things worse by pulling him further down into an emotional pit that he'd rather not be in.

And certainly, there is also the attention-seeker who is going to resist the question, hoping that you might prod further. Hey, it's important to care, but *no one* feels like playing that game.

Rather than ask the question, "What's buggin' ya?," offer the mirrorlike observation: "Sounds like you're upset." If the person wants to come clean about what's bothering him, that's good for you, him, and everybody. If he wants to mope after the statement, well, depending on the circumstances, you likely have something better to do.

Example: "You've been staring at that cup of coffee for a while. It seems as though something is upsetting you."

If You Must Question, Make It Open-Ended

Weak: "Did the situation bother you?"

Powerful: "How did you feel when it happened?"

If the person opens up about a problem and you'd like to help (and at the same time, help the person feel better by discussing the situation), avoid pigeonholing the person with "yes" or "no" types of questions. At best, it might channel the person in limited directions. At worst, a bunch of "yes" or "no" questions make you sound like Nosy Parker.

Ask the person just a few, wide, open-ended questions, and let her do the talking. "What happened?" "How did you feel?" "How are you holding up now?" "What's next for you and your family?"

Again, the philosophy of mirroring subscribes to the notion that these types of questions aren't necessary or ideal. Responding to someone with a nod or with short,

Maximizing Maxim

Asking the right question often leads to the perfect, applicable answer. As French anthropologist Claude Levi-Strauss once said, "The wise man doesn't give the right answers—he poses the right questions."

paraphrased statements is better. But if a question is absolutely necessary to take a fruitful conversation to the next step, make it an open-ended question and allow the person to give details.

Example: "That sounds like a horrible incident. How did you feel when it happened?"

Use Eye Contact

Weak: "Uh-huh," as you look down at the newspaper.

Powerful: "Uh-huh," as you look into the person's eyes.

A good buddy of mine, Roger Vaughan, once sensed that I wasn't really listening to what he had to say. "So, Scott, I figure if we get up early enough, we can catch enough fish to make the trip down to the lake worthwhile."

"Uh-huh," I responded as I continued to read the morning paper.

"And, uh, maybe we'll catch a mermaid or two," he continued, testing me to see if I was listening.

"Uh-huh," I said mindlessly, oblivious to what he was saying but pretending to be courteous.

"Uh oh, Scott, I've caught on fire. Please, please help put me out!"

"Uh-huh."

He laughed, snapped me out of it, and chided me for not showing him the courtesy of listening.

Roger was right. But it goes further. Even if I *had* been listening, I still would have given the impression of not paying attention by staying buried in that paper. By not offering Roger eye contact and a nodding head, I was, in effect, telling him that I wasn't interested.

If someone is speaking to you and you want to convey that you're listening and interested, look at him, nod your head at key points, and keep the newspaper rolled up (and the laptop computer shut).

Example: (As someone says, "I've got this mind-blowing idea for a new kind of car engine.) "Uh-huh," as you nod your head and look into the person's eyes.

Shut Up and Let 'Em Talk

Weak: "Okay, I get it."

Powerful: (Say nothing and allow the person's revelations to play out.)

If, inside your head, you're working on a response while the other person is still speaking, then, with all due respect, you are definitely not employing mirroring or good listening.

Try to listen to the person's full statement, nodding your head and delving into what's being said. Wait a moment before formulating your response: she might start speaking again. If she is going over each little detail of a story, and if you have time to listen, let her do it.

Highlight and Delete

If there's a devil in this universe, then he's the one who makes the phone ring at dinner or during an important conversation. If you're enjoying family time at the table, or if a situation calls for some serious talking and listening on your part, don't allow the phone to interrupt the setting. Turn the ringer off. And while you're at it, turn off your cell phone and encourage others in the room to do so as well. Make the devil work a little harder to interrupt that important give-and-take.

If someone knows that you are actively trying to listen, she is much more likely to give credence to your advice.

Example: (As the person says, "I don't like the way she's always saying bad things about me behind my back.") You say nothing, but as you nod your head, she explains her predicament.

Make 'Em Accept Their Role

Weak: "Why are *other* people to blame?"

Powerful: "What's your role in this dilemma?"

It has been proven time and time again that many, if not most, people feel very much the victims of their own situations. That is, they don't believe that they're responsible—at all—for whatever troubles they've gotten themselves into. It is the rare person, indeed, who owns his own situation, says, "It's on me," and selects a path that reflects his sense of personal accountability.

As with many phrases in this book, this power phrase works by placing the suggestion in a person's mind in a roundabout way. Don't hammer the person by bellowing, "Hey, pal, stop blaming other people and look at yourself." It might feel good (for you) to say that, but it will have very little persuasive value. Have the person recognize his part in the problem by gently asking him how he plays into this current state of affairs. "So, what's your part in all this?" Or perhaps something like, "So where do you come into all this?" Don't ask it in an accusatory, rhetorical manner. Instead, ask it as someone genuinely interested in the other person's role in his own condition.

Of course, the person's response might very well be, "I don't play *any* part in it. I'm an innocent victim." On the other hand, your question might catch him off guard and gently point him in the direction of personal—or at least partial—ownership of the problem. And it might point him toward his own role in forming a solution. See the next item.

Example: "From what you're saying, it sounds as if that committee is a bit dysfunctional. So what's your role in the mayhem?"

Let the Solution Be Theirs

Weak: "Okay. Here's my advice."

Powerful: "What do *you* see as a solution?"

We're quick to jump into advice mode—long before we understand the problem and often without asking whether the person was even looking for advice. It's one side of the world's many current, cultural aversions to listening to people.

That's a shame. Oftentimes, people have the solutions to their own problems: all they have to do is talk them through (after acknowledging the problem exists). When you serve as a sounding board, you make your presence very worthwhile.

Example: "That sounds like a tough problem, and one that's been going on for a long time. What do *you* see as a solution?"

Offer Help

Weak: "When are you going to turn this bad situation around?"

Powerful: "How can I help you make things better?"

Another way of encouraging someone to be a part of the solution instead of part of the problem is to offer help to make it happen. "What can I do to help you make this work?" It sure beats telling someone, "Hey, pal, get your act together."

Making such an offer serves two purposes. First, it openly makes the assumption, without being mean, that there's a problem and a solution. Second, it tells the person, "You're not alone; we can do this together." Even if what you're offering is nothing more than encouragement, it might be enough to make a compelling difference.

This might be a good time to warn against enabling. That is, don't get sucked in to another person's problem to the point where you find yourself solving the problem or doing the work for him. There's a very good chance that you'll wind up getting stuck fixing his next problem as well. The key to effective listening isn't to burden yourself with other people's problems; it's to help people recognize what they have to do for themselves and to do it—and, in the process, to become significant through being beneficial.

Example: "It sounds like your schedule for completing this project needs a bit of reprioritizing. How can I help you rethink and perhaps make it a bit more effective?"

The Least You Need to Know

- We live in a world of cultures that don't know how to listen effectively anymore. And so, that rare person who truly understands and practices the science of good listening has the potential to become very influential.

- Psychologist Carl Rogers in the 1950s promoted the concept of mirroring, in which you reflect what people say to you with paraphrased acknowledgments.

- Often, a statement or an observation draws out more information than a question.

- When the time comes to ask a question, make it an open-ended question—one that allows for a detailed answer.

- If you're not looking at a person while he's speaking, but nodding your head as he makes valid points, you're not really listening to him—at least not in such a way that causes him to open up.

- Suggest in a roundabout way (such as asking about a person's role) that a person should own his or her part of the problem and the solution.

Chapter 11

Redefine the Discussion

In This Chapter

- ◆ Rechanneling the discussion
- ◆ Pointing people in your direction
- ◆ Debating when time permits
- ◆ Saying motivational things
- ◆ Not giving in to groupthink

It's not always about the corporation, or the team, or the other guy. Sometimes the conversation needs to be about *you*—your concerns, your goals, and your requirements. And if the conversation isn't going in that direction, you might think it's the right time to channel it that way.

If a conversation or a meeting—or *any* encounter—isn't going the way you had hoped, there are some ways to place the dialogue on your terms. It's a lot easier to win the game when it begins with *your* rulebook.

Make It About You

Weak: "Here's what you did wrong."

Powerful: "Here's why I feel let down."

People don't like to be criticized. And, as mentioned before, many of them are disinclined to believe that they're wrong in the first place. Sometimes, the trick to convincing someone that he might behave differently is to point out the impact of his actions, especially on you and your sentiments.

> **Highlight and Delete**
>
> When you place something within the perspective of how it's affecting and hurting you, don't dwell on it. Otherwise, the discussion might give the impression that you are being selfish or feeling self-important.

Instead of pointing out how the person did you wrong, tell him how you feel about being let down. He's likely to be persuaded more by your sentiments and impressions than by your accusations.

Example: "Here's why I feel let down. I've been looking forward to this trip for some time, and I haven't seen these old friends of mine for 10 years. For you to change your mind about going at the last minute just breaks my heart. I'm deeply saddened and disappointed."

Keep Walking If You Have To

Weak: "I'm fine. And you?"

Powerful: "I'm great! And it's great to see you!"

There's something very phony about asking someone how she's doing as you're walking by. If you really cared how she was doing, wouldn't you stop to ask? The thing is, many times, you really *don't* have time to stop and ask sincerely how people are doing. And so, you're generally left with two uncomfortable choices. First, you can feign sincerity, ask "How ya doin'?" and move on quickly. Second, you can simply say "Hello" and move on smartly to your next obligation, which seems equally unpleasant. It's uncomfortable and unfriendly, but we all do it.

Allow me to offer an unconventional third option that works. When someone asks "How are you doing?" as you're passing by, don't respond with, "Fine—how about you?" Instead, say "Great, and it's great to see you." That way, you're not asking a question with a potential answer you don't have time for. Plus, you're quickly acknowledging the other person's question/greeting. And, most important, you're telling the person that it's nice to see her. We all like it when people tell us that it's good to have us around—bosses, workmates, family, and friends.

Many times, the person will respond back, "It's good to see you, too." Now isn't that so much better than the empty "How ya doin'?"

Example: ("How ya doin', Scott?") "Good, thanks. It's great to see you." (And off I go to a meeting I'd rather not attend.)

Copy and Paste _____

Try to remember as many names at work as possible. When greeting people, use their names. A person's name is the most important word she hears. And, if you don't have time to talk, you will at least have made a personable impression as you move swiftly along to your obligation.

Say Anything Other Than "Fine"

Weak: "I'm fine. And you?"

Powerful: "I'm on fire!"

Motivational speaker Joel Zeff offers yet a different possibility when someone asks, "How ya doin'?" Zeff's suggestion is to say, "I'm doing fantastic." Or perhaps, "Man, I'm on fire!" The idea is to say anything other than "Fine, thanks" so that the person will remember you and potentially be impressed by your energy and enthusiasm.

I once heard a very successful executive trying to balance work and family say that her goal each and every day was "to change the world but be home in time for dinner."

How's that for another "How ya doin'?" response? "How ya doin', Scott?" "Hey, I'm changing the world, but I'll be home for dinner!"

Example: ("How ya doin', Scott?") "Man, I'm blinded by my own future." (And off I go to yet another meeting I'd rather not attend.)

Say Something Motivational

Weak: "You're right—it's cold out."

Powerful: "I don't need a coat. My love for this place keeps me warm enough!"

In the movie *Master and Commander: The Far Side of the World*, British Royal Navy captain Jack Aubrey (played by Russell Crowe) speaks fondly of Lord Admiral Nelson being offered a coat. "No need for a coat," Nelson ostensibly responded, "my love for king and country keeps me warm."

Granted, sometimes a motivational line comes across as corny and clichéd. But many times, it serves to inspire the people around you and lift the spirits of those who could use a little heartening. "Man, you gotta *love* this life!" "What a glorious day it is today!" "How lucky we are to be alive, here, on this beautiful day!" Sure, they look corny in writing and probably sound corny when you say them. But they sound a lot less corny and have a much stronger impact on the people hearing them than you think they do.

Example: "Every morning when I wake up, the first thing I do is kneel down, say a prayer, and thank God for blessing me with a work team as talented as you good people."

> **Maximizing Maxim**
>
> A kind word, a sincere compliment, or an inspiring thought means a lot to people. Motivation guru Dale Carnegie once said: "When dealing with people, let us remember we are not dealing with creatures of logic. We are dealing with creatures of emotion—creatures bustling with prejudices and motivated by pride and vanity."

Lead 'Em Along with Questions

Weak: "Wow, I enjoy classic movies, too! What's the next one you plan on seeing?"

Also weak: "Wow, I enjoy classic movies, too! Can I take you to one tomorrow night?"

Powerful: "So, am I correct that we both enjoy classic movies? ... Could I tell you about the next one I plan to see?"

Don't jump the gun with an uncomfortable request, such as asking someone out on a date. Instead, use a series of questions to lead the person to an answer that you hope he gives. "So, am I correct that you like vintage rock 'n' roll? Am I correct that you're a fan of Rush? I was thinking of catching their next tour date at the Gebhardt Arena. Could I tell you about my plans?" At any one of these questions, the guy is able to politely bail out without seeming like a bum. Conversely, if he's interested, your questions unhurriedly coax him along, until finally you say, "Would like to join me? I think we'd have a great time."

If you're not sure that someone is going to say yes, it's always easier to allow that person the opportunity to say no without the awkwardness of a flat-out rejection. This series of questions, for example, allows you to ask someone for something where you're still able to work or deal with him comfortably on a daily basis even if he said no to a request.

Example: "So, am I correct that we both enjoy Korean food? And you like traditional Korean cuisine, with the soups, the spices, and the ambiance? Could I tell you about this amazing Korean restaurant not far from here?" (If he says yes to all of those questions and you're interested in asking him out, it seems at this point that he's up for being asked.)

Ask for Contingencies

Weak: "Shouldn't we all just ignore it?"

Powerful: "What if we do nothing?"

When Iraq invaded Kuwait back in the early 1990s, much of the world initially shrugged its collective shoulders. "Oh well," was the general response, "it looks like we're now purchasing our oil from a different proprietor." There were official airs of outrage, but that was about it.

Back in Washington, D.C., President George H. W. Bush faced a group of advisors who were saying pretty much the same thing. But Bush, after a period of silence, asked, "What if we do nothing?" It completely changed the dynamic in the room. And eight months later, an international force ran the Iraqis off Kuwaiti soil.

Before you go along with a group that's choosing to ignore a problem, challenge its members by asking them if they *really* want to do nothing at all. Your challenge may change everything.

Example: "I realize that those dozens of drums of chemicals have been buried out there for years. And I realize that no one is bothering us to test them. But it seems to me there's a potential hazard out there. The question is: What if we do nothing?"

Encourage the Devil's Advocate

Weak: "All in favor?"

Powerful: "What would the devil's advocate say?"

Before you take a vote on an issue that seems like a no-brainer, be sure to encourage a bit more discussion on the subject. Become the *devil's advocate*, or ask someone else to serve as the devil's advocate if you don't feel that it's your place to fill the role. If you're giving into the like-mindedness that's going on around you, then you're really no more influential than the quietest person in the room.

def•i•ni•tion

A **devil's advocate** is the person in a meeting assigned to pick apart an idea that otherwise might not get the scrutiny it requires. By serving as the appointed naysayer, the devil's advocate keeps the meeting from succumbing to *groupthink* (see later on in this chapter).

Look under the hood of this idea before you and your team automatically buy into it. Conferences, in particular, are ugly places where bad ideas take on lives of their own before anyone knows or remembers how they came to be.

Example: "Well, the idea of our township sponsoring a community garden sounds lovely. There are plenty of folks saying they would volunteer, and the food banks would benefit from the produce. Before we move forward, let's look at the drawbacks. What about water supply? What hidden costs are there? What would the devil's advocate say?"

Formalize Your Topic

Weak: "This morning, I'd like to discuss ..."

Powerful: "Joe, would you place this item on your meeting agenda for tomorrow?"

One of the easiest ways to put a discussion on your terms is to have it scheduled that way. That is, if you're going to a meeting where you'd like to talk about something, ask the person who's holding the meeting to place it on his agenda. No bravado—having the item planned is good enough.

Meeting topics take on much more gravity when they are formalized on an agenda. If you're the one holding the meeting, print out the agenda with the important item on it. (Of course, if you run meetings, you should always have a printed agenda to keep things on track.)

Example: "Joe, would you place this item on your meeting agenda for tomorrow? I'd like to discuss this new crossing guard policy. I have concerns regarding the mandatory retirement clause."

Don't Be Pestered When You're Tired

Weak: "Oh, all right."

Powerful: "Ask me tomorrow."

Kids are cunning. They approach you with all kinds of requests just as you're sitting down to watch a great football game or just as you're preparing to settle in for the evening. They inherently understand that, if they can limit the debate, they are more likely to get their way. Clever little rascals, aren't they?

Unfortunately for us, many of these kids never grow up. And, at work and in life, we find ourselves bothered with requests just as we're wrapping up a tough day and ready to go home for dinner. Just this past week, the big boss where I work covered a controversial policy at 3:30 on a Friday afternoon. Was it to stifle disputes and get instant buy-in as people were staring down at the car keys in their hands? Hmmm. Clever little rascal, isn't he?

Of course, you can't tell the big boss, "Hey, some other time." But you *can* say that to everyone else. Hold off discussing something at the end of the day if it merits a sensible amount of deliberation. Refuse to be badgered when you're tired or when you have one foot out the door.

Example: "This seems like a very important decision for all of us. A lot of money and resources and energy are involved. It has been a long day. Please ask me again tomorrow morning, after we've all had a good night's sleep. In fact, stop by my office first thing. We'll head over to the coffee shop and discuss it over java."

Fight Groupthink

Weak: (Silent approval.)

Powerful: "I have a few concerns."

There's nothing weaker than sitting in a meeting, watching a bad idea form a life of its own, and doing nothing about it. History is littered with stories of very intelligent people sitting in the White House allowing bad decisions to take place and quietly buying into those decisions in spite of the horrible national or international ramifications. At that point, *groupthink* had taken over the conference room. Decades later, the people in these meetings would write their memoirs and wonder for their readers how they could have sat there silently as extraordinarily terrible plans were being made.

def•i•ni•tion

> **Groupthink** is a mind-set of compliance that often takes over a group. It was studied as a social concept in the 1970s and 1980s by Yale research psychologist Irving L. Janis. His renowned book on the subject is *Victims of Groupthink: A Psychological Study of Foreign Policy Decisions and Fiascoes* (Houghton Mifflin, 1972).
>
> Groupthink occurs when members of the group quietly give in to conformity and permit decisions to develop without dissent. Once a plan is finalized, these members very often commit themselves to it single-mindedly.

Fight groupthink, and speak up when you're having misgivings. It's the right thing to do, and you won't have to worry about doing penance in your memoirs years from now.

Example: "Uh, not to be a naysayer, but I have a few concerns. For example, if we level the building next door to create more parking, are we certain the ground under the foundation is solid? Has anyone looked into the possibility that there's asbestos in that old building and that we might be getting ourselves into a major, major clean-up expense?"

Take a Stand Against Something Wrong

Weak: "Okay, but don't tell anyone we're doing this."

Powerful: "This isn't right."

One of the weakest things you will ever say in this world is, "I don't like what's going on here, but I'm going to allow it anyway." Essentially, what you're saying is, "I have no control over you or the situation." What you're also saying is, "I have no control over the world around me." And worse still, you might be saying, "I have no morals."

Take a stand against something wrong. Is it going to ruffle some feathers? Sure. But if righteousness is on your side, you may steer the room toward your way of thinking. Besides, it's better to be uncomfortable in a conference room than in a courtroom.

Example: "Listen folks, my principles are getting the best of me here. I just can't see taking taxpayers' money allocated for one thing and secretly channeling it into something else. Any way you slice it, this isn't right."

The Least You Need to Know

- ◆ Sometimes it pays to address a point of disagreement from the perspective of how it's affecting you and your feelings. Instead of offering accusations, explain the disappointment from your angle.

- ◆ Corny, high-energy sayings often work to motivate others. They sound a lot less corny to the people hearing them.

◆ Suggest that something must be done by asking what might happen if nothing is done.

◆ Don't ask people how they're doing if you don't have caring, effective listening time for their responses. And don't address a request at the end of the day when you're tired.

◆ If you are very interested in having something discussed, ask that it be placed on the next meeting agenda.

◆ Fight groupthink by seriously scrutinizing an idea instead of mindlessly going along with it—display your strength by taking a stand against something that is wrong.

Chapter 12

Lose the Battle, but Win the War

In This Chapter

- ◆ Granting the small win
- ◆ Acknowledging another person's line of reasoning
- ◆ Recognizing other people's passion
- ◆ Basing an argument on calmness and truth
- ◆ Emphasizing what others will gain

Take one step back but two steps forward. That's how not only life and success work: it's also how battle works. Giving up one city block to take control of the entire downtown marketplace—that's what successful urban warfare is all about.

If you dig in early during a discussion and refuse to make any concessions, you might win a tiny toehold in the argument, but not much else. And if you're looking to change someone's attitude or convince that person to support you in a grander scheme, you're probably in for a disappointment.

wer words may seem compromising. But these expressions, in
ct, don't yield much. They simply concede a small piece of ground to
set you up for long-term success.

Concede the Small Point

Weak: "Maybe you're right, but …"

Powerful: "I stand corrected."

Why argue over a small point if there's something bigger around the
corner that you need to put right? Simply give in by saying, "You're
probably right," and move on to the bigger issue. Even if you know the
person's facts are wrong, if he's pointed in your general philosophical
direction, there's no reason to be fastidious. Concede. That doesn't
mean you give up or lose. It means you yield, usually in the spirit of
compromise. And when you do concede, offer the concession sincerely,
then continue with friendlier items.

> **Maximizing Maxim**
>
> In his milestone work *How to Win Friends and Influence People*
> (Pocket Books, 1990), Dale Carnegie suggests that it's impossible
> to win an argument. He proposed that 90 percent of the time, people
> become more entrenched than ever after an argument. "You can't win an
> argument," Carnegie advises. "You can't because if you lose it, you lose
> it; and if you win it, you lose it."

"Well, Scott, you know that people speak seven different dialects of
Latin in Latin America."

"They do? Well, I stand corrected. I thought it was a bit of a dead
language. But you may be right. So let's talk about that academic conference in Rio de Janeiro you were thinking about sending me to!"

Example: (After someone says, "We've tried that. It didn't work.")
"I stand corrected. I didn't know that we had tried something similar in
the past. If you tried it before, I assume you agree with the philosophy
behind the plan. Do you have any ideas regarding a different plan that
might get us to the same point?"

Don't Concede What Can Be Changed

Weak: "It is what it is ..."

Powerful: "Let's work on changing the things we can."

I guess I understand the concept behind "It is what it is." The phrase essentially means "Let's accept it and move on." And indeed, there's something very powerful about accepting the things you cannot change. If you concentrate your efforts and your life stress only on those things that are reasonably changeable, then you remove all kinds of wasted energy and anxiety from your life.

The deal with "It is what it is" is twofold: 1) It's one of the most over-used phrases currently in use; and 2) It has a certain fatalistic tone to it. Instead of sounding so defeatist, suggest to the team that you channel your efforts toward something important and movable.

Example: "Clearly we can't get rid of all the crime in the city. But let's concentrate on the rash of robberies that have taken place on Hooligan Street and Hoodlum Street. We believe that with some added lighting, a few extra foot police, and this new citizens' patrol program, we can make a dramatic difference. Let's work on changing the things we can."

 Copy and Paste _____

There's much wisdom to be gained from the Serenity Prayer, which appropriately concludes most 12-step addiction-recovery meetings. "God, grant me the serenity to accept the things I cannot change, the courage to change the things I can, and the wisdom to know the difference."

Don't Tell 'Em They're Crazy

Weak: "You're crazy."

Powerful: "I see your point."

One of my favorite *X-Files* episodes includes a scene with the late, great Peter Boyle playing Clyde Bruckman. At one point, a serial killer asks Bruckman, "Why have I done them?"

"Don't you understand yet, son?" Bruckman returns rhetorically. "Don't you get it? You do the things you do because you're a homicidal maniac."

A look of understanding washes over the killer's face. "That *does* explain a lot, doesn't it?"

Ah, the wonders of television. Reality, however, is much different. The likelihood of convincing someone that he's crazy is, well, crazy in itself. Nutty people with nutty ideas (or even ordinary people with nutty ideas) tend not to pay attention to the reasoned folks.

Even if you *were* able to convince someone that his idea was crazy, what good would it do? He'd likely feel humiliated and bitter. And the next time he had a really *good* idea, you're the last person with whom he would share it.

Instead of telling someone that his idea is nuts, acknowledge the good thoughts behind the idea, and see if you can form a bridge between his good thoughts and a plan that makes a little more practical sense.

Example: "I see your point, Lucy. Cats really *are* a nuisance in this town. But I'm a little concerned about the public outcry your proposed feline tannery would create. Perhaps there's a way you could channel your energy toward expanding, say, the volunteer program at the local animal shelter."

Don't Offer Excuses

Weak: "Here are the reasons I couldn't finish that task."

Powerful: "No excuses."

Copy and Paste

West Point cadets are taught early in their military training to say, "No excuse, sir," rather than to offer a string of weak explanations.

Sure, there are all kinds of extenuating circumstances related to why you're late in completing a project. But truth be told, people don't care. Not much, anyway. And unless your excuse involves stumbling across a new dimension into another universe, they probably don't want to hear your excuses.

In Chapter 13, I discuss phrases that help keep you from sounding like a victim. Again, we all have good reasons for being late—life has a funny way of getting in the way. But really, if you say, "Sorry for being late—no excuses," people will appreciate your ownership of the delay.

Example: "Yes, ma'am, I am late with the second half of this book's manuscript. No excuses. Just don't hate me for being beautiful!"

Don't Build a Conversation on a Lie

Weak: "That's a lie, and I can prove it. Gotcha!"

Powerful: "Sorry, but I don't believe that's true at all. I suppose we're done here for now."

There are really very few ways a discussion can go if you don't believe the statements that form the foundation of the dialogue. Building a conversation or a negotiation on top of a blatant lie doesn't seem good for anyone.

You could address the lie or ask a series of questions in an attempt to catch the person, but to what end? The inquisition and—if you're wrong—the admission of error can take place later on. It's better to stop wasting everyone's time (most important, your own), explain why you're ending the discussion, and return to the topic some other time. If the person is proven to be dishonest, then there's no reason to return to the table.

Example: "Sorry, but I don't believe those projected expenses are true. They just don't mesh with anything that our neutral, nonbidding consultants have proposed. I suppose we're done here for now."

Cool Off

Weak: "You're being loud, mean, and abusive, but I can be even *more* loud, mean, and abusive."

Powerful: "Why don't we all take a breather, cool down, and try this again later today or tomorrow?"

Hey, I can yell and curse with the best of them. But I'm the first to admit that when I do so, it weakens me as a person and it weakens my influence within any particular group. The truly powerful person is the one who refuses to be sucked in by the emotions and instead seeks to buffer highly charged people before they get out of hand.

Of course, I'm not suggesting that you stand between two drunks ready to brawl. But if a conference room is losing its civility, it's best to end things, let cooler heads prevail, and broach the topic again some other time.

Example: "Clearly, this proposed highway off-ramp is an emotional issue for everyone, and it's getting pretty loud in here. Why don't we all take a breather, cool down, and try this again later today or tomorrow? Why don't we agree not to hunt each other down in the hallway or the parking lot? Let's stay away from one another and calm down until tomorrow."

Act as If You Can Do Something

Weak: "Hey, pal, what do you want from *me*?"

Powerful: "What would make this situation right for you?"

People don't necessarily approach you with a distressing problem because they expect you to do something. They might just want to talk. But if you project yourself as helpless, it creates an uneasy conversation in which the more she tries to tell you the problem, the more you helplessly beg off the topic. It makes you look both uncaring and feeble, even if unfairly so.

A better way to handle such a person is to pretend for a second that you are theoretically able to do something about whatever is anguishing this person. "I hear you," you respond. "So what would make this situation right for you?" You might be surprised to hear the person say, "Well, nothing, I suppose. And I know I'm burdening you with this, even though there's little you can do about it. Thanks for allowing me to vent."

Or you may, in typical Rogerian fashion (see Chapter 10), serve as a sounding board and springboard for her to find her own solution. It was probably right there all along. It's also worth mentioning here that if the person seems terribly traumatized, you should recommend counseling. Even the most powerful, unwavering people need a mental health fine-tuning now and then.

Example: "It sounds as if you're troubled by the judge's decision. And I understand the appeals have run out as well. What would make this situation right for you?"

Point Out the Passion

Weak: "You're wrong."

Powerful: "Clearly this is something that you're passionate about. How do you know so much about it?"

"You're wrong, you're wrong, you're wrong."

"Well, since you put it that way, clearly I can see that I'm wrong. I'd better calm down and be on my way." Have you ever heard a conversation go that way before? Neither have I.

Instead of banging heads with someone over whether or not she's wrong, why not change the subject just a bit? Acknowledge the person's passion on the subject and have her talk about herself. People love to talk about themselves. When you allow them to do so, they often lower their defenses.

If a neighbor is complaining that you don't mow your lawn often enough, compliment her lawn and ask how she keeps it so manicured. She'll likely tell you about how she edges, cross-cuts, and fertilizes that green carpet. The subject isn't forgotten, but the tone is a lot friendlier.

Example: "So, you believe I'm displaying the American flag incorrectly? Hmmm. Well, clearly this is something that you're passionate about. Where did you learn so much about flying the flag?"

Show Gratitude for the Effort

Weak: "Why can't you be more like Matt?"

Powerful: "Thanks for all you do."

If you want to weaken your position in your family, at your workplace, or among your group of friends, make sure to appraise someone's performance against the accomplishments of someone who does it better. There's nothing more disheartening than to work your butt off, only to have someone brush off your efforts as inferior to those of someone else. It is the ultimate de-motivator.

Instead of comparing someone to someone else, thank that person for all he does and point out the positive parts of what he has done. Compare someone's accomplishments to what he has done in the past, or to some new higher standard he has set for himself. Encourage; don't be an ungrateful nag.

Highlight and Delete

Don't ever end a thank-you with a "but." For example: "Thanks sincerely for the effort, but you didn't ..." It will feel as if you never said thanks at all. Instead, ask for the unfinished task, note its completion, and end with a heartfelt "Thanks so much."

Example: "Thanks for all you do around here, Andy. I noticed your new method for keeping a ledger. It looks like it works pretty much the way you said it would: easier, more streamlined, and with more information for the morning meeting. Nice job."

Don't Lie for Anyone

Weak: "Okay, what lie do you want me to tell?"

Powerful: "Sorry, but I'm not going to lie for you."

At the outset, it seems like the appropriate thing to do: a friend asks you to lie for her. And that's what friends do, right? They cover for each other, right?

Wrong.

I respectfully suggest that the second someone asks you to lie for her, she has stopped being your friend. At that point, she's just someone trying to exploit you and insult your sense of friendship. If she were a true friend, she wouldn't be pulling you down into the hole she has dug for herself.

There is strong, long-term value in refusing to lie for others. A quick look at many notorious crimes throughout history suggests that the cover-up was just as damaging, if not more so, to the people involved. One of the most powerful phrases you'll ever use is, "Sorry, but I won't lie for you."

Example: "So, you want me to tell the police that you were here last night? Sorry, friend, but I'm not going to lie for you. I've got a wife and kids to take care of, and the last thing I need is to get drawn into legal trouble. If you ever want to talk about what you're in trouble for, let me know."

Remind Them of Their Stake

Weak: "Here's what's in it for me."

Powerful: "Here's what's in it for you."

People don't want to hear about your win-win scenario. What they really want to hear about is *their* win-win scenario. In other words, they want to know what's in it for them: everything else is just fluff.

Highlight and Delete

If you're someone who likes change just for the sake of change, you've got a tough sale ahead of you. People are generally hard-wired for habit, and they are generally hostile toward change. If a change is necessary, emphasize the benefits of the change and the big-picture reasons behind it. If the change is simply to try something different, I wish you the best of luck.

Even if what you're proposing is largely for your benefit, try to tailor the presentation as much as possible toward the people who have to approve it. Don't lie, of course. But accentuate the positive for those hearing and scrutinizing your grand plan.

Example: "Here's what's in it for you. This new store will bring convenience, jobs, and more shoppers to other stores in the area. It will also benefit the town itself by bringing in more revenue, more income tax dollars, and, from the store itself, more property tax dollars. Your town will greatly benefit from the construction of this new store."

The Least You Need to Know

◆ Don't get hung up on a small point. Concede the point and move on, especially if the other person is headed in your general philosophical direction.

◆ Concentrate your thoughts and your words on those things that are reasonably achievable, thus eliminating wasted energy and anxiety.

◆ There are times when it's best to end a discussion altogether, such as when you believe someone is lying or when the people in the room are losing their cool.

◆ If you want to turn someone's complaints into a positive thing, acknowledge his passion and have him start talking about himself and why he's passionate about such a thing. You just might wind up having a friend and advocate for life.

◆ De-emphasize your own role and stress to your listeners what *they* will get out of a situation; by pointing out the benefits to other people, you may bring those other people around to your way of thinking.

Part **4**

Words and Expressions to Avoid

While referencing powerful words and phrases, it's worth examining those expressions that do the opposite—weaken you and your arguments. Fortunately, if you can spot a weak word, you can easily replace it.

Some words and phrases are flimsy and victimlike. When you use them, you sound like someone who has lost control of the situation and perhaps even of life. Replace these expressions with ones that give off the air that you're in charge of your existence and responsible for your surroundings.

There are also words that come off as way too trendy and soon-to-be clichéd. The cool (may I say "cool"?) thing about most power words is that they are enduring and impervious to fads.

WELL, HIGGINS... ALTHOUGH THIS LETTER IS POWERFUL AND CONCISE, IT'S NOT REALLY THE STYLE WE WERE LOOKING FOR!

SIGN THE CONTRACT OR ELSE!

BARR

Chapter 13

Don't Be a Victim

In This Chapter

- ◆ Owning the problem
- ◆ Saying no to excuses
- ◆ Turning it around
- ◆ Painting it positive
- ◆ Limiting your demands

It seems as if everyone is a victim these days. Sure, life's tough, and the world's full of people who, for whatever odd reasons, would love to see you fail. But why let these tormenters get the best of you? By refusing to be a victim, you throw their intimidation right back at them.

Here are some expressions that help you present yourself as very much in charge of your life and able to affect what happens around you. And because they'll know you're in charge of yourself, they might—if you so choose—allow you to be in charge of them as well. Don't be a victim. Seize the day!

Quit Yer Whining

Avoid: "I'm the victim here."

Instead: "We need to make this right."

"This organization's got me down. I feel very much victimized by recent events." If you feel as if you've been wronged, it's certainly reasonable for you to seek justice. However, you're much more likely to reach this reckoning if you do so from an inner sense of empowerment, as opposed to the feeble feeling of victimhood.

Example: "I'm not crazy about what's going on here, but let's talk this through. We need to make this right."

> **Maximizing Maxim** _____
>
> Chinese philosopher Confucius had the right idea when it came to owning one's mistakes. He suggested that the cover-up was usually much more damaging than the initial mistake. Confucius said: "Be not ashamed of mistakes and thus make them crimes."

Own Up to It

Avoid: "It was done."

Instead: "I did it."

I've already mentioned the weak nature of writing things in the passive voice. But it merits another mention. Don't say, "Mistakes were made." Own your errors, tell people you've learned from them, and insist that they won't happen again.

Tell people, "I own that boo-boo, and that's a lick on me." And then go about the business of being the successful person you are.

Example: "Yes, I made the scheduling error. It won't happen again."

Don't Blame the Other Guy

Avoid: "It was Joe's fault."

Instead: "There are some things we all could have done differently."

Okay, so Joe screwed up royally. Many people know it—but not everyone. And so, when accusations begin to fly, it's understandable that, in a moment of self-preservation, you want to tell the world that it's Joe's fault and not yours.

There are some drawbacks to this idea. First, if you sound overprotective of yourself, you also sound feeble. Also, following the concept of projecting compliments (see Chapter 17), if you sharply criticize others, people will relate the criticism more to you than to Joe. Unfair, but true. And finally, if you don't allow Joe the opportunity to "save face," he'll resent you for a very long time. Instead, address mistakes from the standpoint of what the group might do better next time.

Example: "I think you'll agree that the presentation didn't go well. It seems to me that there are some things we all could have done differently. Maybe after a good night's sleep we could discuss how to make that whole production better."

 Copy and Paste _____

The truly confident leader shares compliments ("Thanks for your kind thoughts—I'll let the people who put the project together know") but accepts criticism ("I'm responsible—it happened on my watch").

Yes, It *Is* Your Problem

Avoid: "That's not my problem."

Instead: "How might we go about fixing this?

When someone says, "That not my problem" or "That's not my job," it sounds so defensive and, in many cases, so lazy that the statement puts the person in anything but a position of power. Sure, he may be in control in the sense that he doesn't have to handle that particular problem. But if he wants to cocoon himself in a shield of limited job descriptions, he's going to isolate himself in that cocoon.

Instead of reminding others what you will and won't take care of, be a leader by looking at any problem from the vantage point of a problem solver. It won't be forgotten.

Example: "I'm not sure I can help, but I'm willing to offer a hand. How might we go about fixing this? What do you think needs to happen?"

It's What You Make It

Avoid: "It has been a rough day."

Instead: "I'm going to seize the day!"

"Carpe diem," as the Roman poet Horace wrote in *The Odes*. The phrase is Latin for "seize the day." Writes Horace: "How much better to endure whatever will be."

There comes a point during a particularly bad time when you need to pull a Sylvester Stallone in *Rocky III*, look in the mirror, and get your "Eye of the Tiger" going. That is, sometimes you need to tell yourself who's running your life. That's right—you are. So don't tell everyone how tough your day or week has been. They either don't care or they're happy to see another person as miserable as they are. Instead, loudly proclaim that you are seizing the day!

Example: "Well, either I'm going to keep letting this day run me, or *I'm* going run *it*. Doggone it, I'm going to seize the day! Let's turn this around!"

Maybe It's 'Cause Karma Loves You

Avoid: "Why do bad things always happen to me?"

Instead: "I'm still standing."

I don't want to dwell on karma or destiny. But it certainly is worth noting here that, if you believe the angels are deliberately throwing a series of bad events your way, it's better to acknowledge their control than to lament to others about your sorry luck. You'll sound more in control, and the angels, sensing that they're not going to get to you, might back off. (Of course, privately, you might want to ask them for the strength to endure.)

Example: "Wow, has this been a tough week. Oh well, we're still standing."

Highlight and Delete _____

Whether your religion involves karma or angels or whatever, don't use religion as leverage for getting your way in a diverse group. People will resent it. And if they sense that you're only using the morality as a power device, they will forever question your genuineness.

Never Say Never

Avoid: "We'll never be able to do that."

Instead: "Yes, we can."

I have many heroes at both extremes of the U.S. political spectrum. But from the somewhat narrow viewpoint of inspiration by rhetoric, no one does it much better than President Barack Obama.

Would it be silly to suggest that his mantra "Yes, we can" got him elected? Probably. But the speeches he built around that unadorned phrase made a big impact. I remember a colleague of mine talking about Obama's stump speech on C-SPAN, only a few weeks after Obama had declared his candidacy. My colleague's bold prediction: "Last night, I heard our next president speak on television."

Don't be negative. And never say never. Tell your team, in words of a similar fashion, that yes, you can achieve big, bold goals.

Example: "Can we turn things around? Yes, we can! Can we make this a better place to live? Yes, we can!"

Don't Blame Traffic

Avoid: "Traffic was bad."

Instead: "Sorry I'm late."

At Fort Bragg, North Carolina, in the late 1980s, the junior officers were told never to blame traffic or car trouble for being late for a meeting or a muster. In fact, officers using that excuse were forced to attend traffic classes and auto maintenance courses.

Did these officers need such courses? No. They were just being punished for using a lame excuse. If the retribution was a bit harsh, the lesson wasn't; no one wants to hear your pathetic explanations, especially if you kept a room full of people waiting. It is best to say you're sorry and that it won't happen again. And then live up to the promise.

Example: "Sorry I'm late. It won't happen again."

Again, I Say, Never Say Never

Avoid: "This will *never* get better."

Instead: "This is just the downhill part of the rollercoaster."

There is something soothing and reassuring about knowing that things eventually will get better. And let's face it, they almost always do. To present yourself as someone of authority, you must remind people that it will happen.

Instead of victimizing yourself by predicting nothing but horrible things down the road, repeat the idea that life is cyclical and that, as King Solomon once observed, "This too shall pass."

Example: "Well, life has its ups and downs. This is just the downhill part of the rollercoaster. We'll get past it soon enough."

"But" Means "I Disagree"

Avoid: "Yes, but …"

Instead: "Hmmm …"

When you say, "Yes, but," you probably mean the "but" part and you probably *don't* mean the "yes" part. When someone says, "Yes, but," what he's really doing is interrupting. It's very likely he hasn't really heard a word the other person has said. "Yes, but" pries its way into the other person's thoughts, turning a conversation into a talking give-and-give that involves little or no listening.

Turn off the whininess. Show your maturity and control by staying quiet long enough to let the other person talk. In fact, go a step further and really listen to what is being said. There's at least a theoretical possibility that the other person is partially right and you're partially wrong. Say, "Hmmm." Nod your head. Show some respect for the opposing view.

Example: "So you think I could have done that better. Hmmm ..."

Use the Magic of Three

Avoid: "Here's my list of 20 demands."

Instead: "Here are three things we could be doing better."

Okay, so you have the attention of someone who can bring about a change in your situation. Should you ramble on for half an hour with a litany of demands, or should you limit yourself to the three things you find most pressing? I recommend the shorter list. Important people are busy and, with respect, short of attention span. Three items will garner a response.

I'm not sure what it is about lists of three that make them so magical. The Bible is full of trios and trilogies. The quintessential argumentative essay has three supporting paragraphs. In most jokes, the punch line happens at the third incident. It's a mystery to me. But in any case, if you have the ear of a major decision-maker, limit your list of requests to three.

Example: "I stand here before you today with some thoughts on dramatically improving how we put together our business plans and how we do business throughout each month. Here are three things that we could be doing better."

The Least You Need to Know

- ◆ You're more likely to find justice from the inner sense of empowerment than from the weak feeling of victimhood.

- ◆ Instead of shielding yourself from any and all problems, define yourself as a leader by identifying yourself as a potential problem-solver.

- ◆ Don't be a fortune-teller of eternal misery. Instead, seize the day and control the day—don't let the day run you.

◆ Never tell a group that something can't happen. Instead, write a mantra and repeat it—remind those around you, over and over again, that big goals are possible.

◆ No one wants to hear your excuses for not getting something done, even if the reasons are legitimate. If you have kept people waiting, say you're sorry and that it won't happen again.

14

Don't Use "Flavor of the Day" Expressions

In This Chapter

♦ Using more durable phrases

♦ Avoiding cute, modish sayings

♦ Not stating the obvious

♦ Not blaming headquarters

♦ Shunning dumb business clichés

A cliché is a phrase that might have been clever at one time (you know this from reading Chapter 4), but now it is overused and tired to the point where its use hinders rather than helps your communication. The opposite of a cliché is an in-vogue phrase, which has the sound of something that is so hip and so stylish as to be nauseating.

Many of the following phrases are, relatively speaking, not old enough to fall under the category of cliché. But they are truly revolting—probably my least favorite phrases ever. These "flavor of the day" expressions will hopefully disappear soon, but I doubt it: I hate them so much that I can only assume they'll be around for a while.

In no particular order, here are some real humdinger phrases to avoid. Replace them with genuine, enduring power words and phrases.

Forget the Mouse

Avoid: "Let's build a better mousetrap."

Instead: "Let's try a solution that's imaginative."

This phrase addresses the idea that perhaps people in business should occasionally be ingenious or clever. What a novel notion!

There's nothing wrong with asking people to (no, not think outside the box) push the limits of their imaginations. But using such a goofy phrase as "build a better mousetrap" isn't a very inspired way to ask people to be inspired.

Example: "Maybe it's time that we took a fresh look at our standard operating procedures. Let's try a solution that's bold and imaginative."

Forget the Twenty Cents

Avoid: "Paradigm shift."

Instead: "A complete redefining of the issue."

I've mentioned the word *paradigm* before. But the phrase "paradigm shift" really gets under my nails. A "paradigm shift" occurs when the laws and concepts within a particular school of thought are completely changed. For example, Albert Einstein's Theory of Relativity completely changed the way people approached physics and the universe.

Instead of using a phrase that only a secret group of academics (with their decoder rings in hand) understands, suggest that something entirely redefines an issue. Considering how quickly information is growing and being transmitted or communicated these days, this could apply to just about anything.

Example: "Things are really moving fast in the field of credit card security. Just in the last five years, we've seen a complete redefining of the issues and what constitutes secure usage."

Yes, We All Heard It

Avoid: "I heard *that*!"

Instead: "I agree!"

"Man, I heard *that*!" I guess there's nothing wrong with the occasional use of slang, or nonstandard language. But this one seems to belong to those who are going along with the crowd, rather than to the person who is trying to persuade or lead the crowd.

> ## Maximizing Maxim
>
> Not all colloquial speech is bad. American writer and poet Carl Sandburg suggested that flavor-of-the-day speech had a special role. "Slang is a language," he wrote, "that rolls up its sleeves, spits on its hands, and goes to work!"

I suggest that a strong "Here, here!" or "Agreed!" conveys a much stronger image than, "I heard *that*!" Besides, this phrase seems fadlike enough that, down the road, when the minutes of a meeting are being read back, your saying "I heard that!" will seem outmoded and embarrassing.

Example: "I agree! The hotel hosting that conference could have done lots of things better. I felt poorly treated from start to finish."

The Only Word That Goes with "Grasp"

Avoid: "We're grasping at straws."

Instead: "We're starting to sound desperate."

Do we grasp at anything other than at straws? I suppose we attempt to grasp a concept. Or grasp for air. Oops, sorry, that's "gasp!"

The phrase "grasping at straws" is, truth be told, several hundred years old and so, strictly speaking, not really a flavor-of-the-day phrase. It comes from the saying that a drowning man will grasp at anything to survive, even a straw, as unlikely as that might be to save him.

But the phrase seems to have gained a second (or third, or fourth) wind in recent years. It seems to be showing up everywhere. I suggest that, if things are desperate and people are considering unlikely options, rather than use this weak phrase, just say, "We're starting to sound desperate."

Example: "Clearly, our options are limited, and we're starting to sound desperate. Perhaps our best course of action is the most obvious course: secure our assets, pay our bills, and stop trying to speculate our way out of a tough financial situation."

Better to Raise Cain

Avoid: "Raise the bar."

Instead: "Increase expectations."

About 100 years ago, I sold car phones for a living. No, not the sleek wireless phones. These were the old-fashioned box phones with 3 watts of power that sat on the passenger seats of many businesspeople on the go. I made pretty good money selling those things.

Anyway, whenever I got into the groove of selling my phone quota for a certain salary, the company increased my quota. They never said out loud, "We're increasing your quota" or worse, "We're lowering your pay." What they said was, "We're going to raise the bar."

Copy and Paste

If you're in charge of people, keep your e-mails brief, simple, and few in number. Electronic communication is truly a medium where more is less.

The phrase seemed to fade for a while, but it's back again. If you're increasing the expectations of your sales force or anyone else for that matter, simply say so. "We believe this product is gaining market interest, and we're increasing our expectations of you, the salesperson." That's a lot easier to handle than "We're raising the bar."

Example: "Now that we have settled into a comfortable manufacturing process, we're going to have to speed up these machines a bit. They were designed to handle more output, and we need to increase our expectations of what we can make them produce on any given day."

No One Wants a Fringe Competency

Avoid: "Core competencies."

Instead: "What we're most passionate about and what we do best."

"We need to return to our core competencies." Is it possible to hear that in a meeting without laughing aloud (which, of course, I don't recommend)?

A core competency, simple enough, is something a company does that draws business and sets it apart from its competitors. Granted, some companies, in the spirit of trying new things, stray from what they're superior at. But if it's time to return to those things, why not just say so? Using such a silly term does not make you sound important. I humbly suggest that it's just the opposite.

Example: "Although there was a time where we had the assets and the long-term plan to stretch outside our regular markets, it seems that we're in a financial position now where we need to return to what we do best and what we've always been the most passionate about."

Wouldn't the Selfish Approach Be Better?

Avoid: "We need to take a team approach."

Instead: (Nothing. You should already be looking at it that way.)

The "team approach" is another soybeanlike filler phrase that means nothing at all. The super-cynical person might say that when a boss says "team approach," what she means is, "Oops, I made a mistake, and so I'm going to pull as many of you into being blamed as I can!"

The less cynical person might say that "team approach" simply means pulling all interested parties into the decision-making and implementation processes. Sounds like good management to me. But there's no need to call it anything: the effective manager should have been keeping everyone involved (and accountable) all along.

Example: "Thanks for what you're contributing to this team. I appreciate it." (And then nothing more. If you have something else to talk about regarding that person's work ethic, reference it in another way, or see your boss.)

Don't Blame HQ

Avoid: "Here's a new directive from on high."

Instead: "There's a new policy. Let's see how it will apply to us."

Although it's tempting to blame everything on the headquarters way up the food chain, it displays too much helplessness when every new policy is given the eye-rolling "from on high" treatment. Remember that loyalty up the chain of command should equal loyalty *down* the chain.

Rather than dismissing or apologizing for the new policy straight away, suggest that team members take some time to evaluate how the policy might affect them. This consideration includes determining how hard and fast the policy is, how much input your team had in helping to set the policy, and how steeped in reality the policy is.

Example: "There's a new policy involving reimbursement for official travel. At first glance, it doesn't seem to bode well for our department. But let's comb through it and see how it will apply to us."

Don't Forget the Results Show

Avoid: "Results-driven."

Instead: "Concentrated on essentials."

Yet another meaningless phrase is "results-driven." Why do anything if it's not expected to generate results? And yet this phrase has truly reached great flavor-of-the-day heights.

More often than not, the phrase is probably used to imply that long-term, hit-and-miss strategies are off the table, and that only more vital plans are to be used. In other words, the new business plan concentrates on essentials. So say that.

Highlight and Delete

Be careful. Business jargon has a very short shelf life. A seemingly intellectual business phrase today can be the predictable joke tomorrow.

Example: "What we need to do during this tough time is to put together a plan that is concentrated on the essentials. We need to make sure that our program, for now, is short-term and based on preserving the part of the market we currently hold. Let's make a point of doing what we do best and see how this economic downturn is going to affect our product line."

Don't Overemphasize the Big Picture

Avoid: "30,000-foot view."

Instead: "Not getting hung up on minutiae."

Sure the devil is in the details, but even big items get tiny from 30,000 feet up. How did that particular height become so trendy, anyway?

Sure, I get it. Too much attention to tiny details is a bad thing. Broadstroke business planners shouldn't be getting hung up on minutiae. So say that.

Example: "Let's put together the bigger plan for now. We don't want to get hung up on minutiae at this particular meeting. After we're done locking in the strategy, we'll put together a few field committees to work out the details."

Don't Ask Your Customers to Call

Avoid: "Please don't hesitate to call."

Instead: "Thanks so much for all your good faith. I will check up on you in a week or so."

Some salesmen sayings are courteous and necessary. Others are just obnoxious. "Don't hesitate to call" is one of the obnoxious ones. If you just purchased a one-year equipment-service agreement and no one is showing up for the service, would you hesitate to call?

A better thing to say would be, "I'll call." As in, "Thank you for your business. I'll call within the next couple of days to make sure you're happy with your purchase." Those are power words. And it's good business.

Example: "Thanks so much for all your good faith. Your shipment ought to arrive in a couple of days. I'll check up a day or two after that to see if you need anything or if you have any concerns."

The Least You Need to Know

- Power words have a certain enduring quality to them that take them out of the realm of trendy expressions, jargon, or slang.

- Avoid jargon if your communication includes people outside a very tight and exclusive professional circle.

- Be careful of business jargon—by its nature, it tends to become obsolete quickly. An insightful term today can seem old, simplistic, and silly tomorrow.

- Watch for trendy expressions that sound good initially but, upon further inspection, really say nothing at all.

- Straightforward phrases and directions are always favored over flavor-of-the-day expressions.

Chapter 15

Don't Attack People

In This Chapter

- ◆ Getting past the argument
- ◆ Avoiding the cheap shot
- ◆ The value of courtesy
- ◆ Steering clear of fortune-telling
- ◆ Having people join your team

If there's a plus side to verbally attacking people, you won't meet too many powerful folks who know what it is. Truly influential people understand the merits of avoiding confrontation whenever possible and diving headfirst into conciliation and cooperation.

Avoid the following phrases out of respect for the idea that you'll never win a battle of personalities head-on. Don't attack people. Instead, extend a hand and get them on your side.

Get Past the Right-or-Wrong Angle

Avoid: "Here's why you're wrong."

Instead: "You make a good point. Have you ever thought about …?"

More times than not, there's good intention behind a somewhat dismal idea. Instead of picking apart the idea, why not praise the intention? Then segue into whatever part of the plan has enough merit to discuss or whatever part of it might bridge over to something more practical.

I should point out here that you shouldn't be too quick to degrade someone's idea. Many innovative and worthwhile proposals seem batty at first. Dig a little deeper before you're completely certain the other person is wrong. Maybe the wrong one is you.

Example: "You make a good point regarding the need for more funding. Have you ever thought about moving money from one part of the project to fund another part?"

Try to Relate

Avoid: "I don't know what you're talking about."

Instead: "I can only imagine how you must feel."

When someone tells you something that makes little sense to you or doesn't involve you at all, it's tempting to say, "Hey pal, I don't know what you're talking about." Man, that's a pretty cold hand to hold up to someone's face.

> **Maximizing Maxim**
>
> Etiquette author Emily Post once suggested that understanding and appreciating others' feelings is the ultimate exercise in protocol. "Manners are a sensitive awareness of the feelings of others," she wrote. "If you have that awareness, you have good manners, no matter what fork you use."

If the person looks anguished over what she's telling you, try a little bit of empathy and see if you can move on from there. If the person opens up, you might get to the message she's trying to relate. And if she needs to vent and talk about her distress, you're doing someone a good deed by listening.

Example: "It sounds as if you're upset over how the annual bonuses were calculated. I'm not part of the bonus system at this company, but I can imagine how you must feel."

Be Tactful

Avoid: "That was boring."

Instead: "That was nice, but maybe not for me."

I don't recommend ever lying about anything; lies are too difficult to manage, and the truth always comes out. Besides, lying is wrong.

However, a little bit of social *tact* goes a long way. If someone spends any effort or money at all trying to entertain you, you should be gracious enough not to say what you really thought of the experience. "Poetry and guitars? You gotta be kiddin' me!" Instead try, "Hmmm, that reminded me of my younger, more freewheeling days. Thanks for bringing back those memories."

def•i•ni•tion

> **Tact** is a sense of what to say or how to act in order not to offend others. Although it involves being less than brutally honest, being tactful is generally not synonymous with being deceitful.

If you're afraid of being invited again to something you didn't enjoy, tell the person that it was nice but not really for you.

Example: "That roller skating–bingo parlor was really something different. Very high-energy. Maybe not for me, though. I kept thinking I was going to throw my back out every time they said B-4."

I Heard a Rumor That You Tell Rumors

Avoid: "Want to hear a rumor about Joe?"

Instead: (Nothing. If you listen to or tell rumors, you'll fall victim to them.)

I love a good rumor. It really perks up an otherwise humdrum day at the office. There's just one problem: whenever I'm listening to a rumor, I can't stop thinking that there's another one being told down the hallway—about me! And just like the person I'm hearing about who can't defend herself, I can't defend myself down the hallway.

Rumors are generally poison—for the workplace and for the people whose names are involved. One more thing: if someone knows you'll listen to a rumor about others, she knows you'll also listen to a rumor about her. And from the position of influence and friendship, you become weaker.

Example: (Someone asks you, "Did you hear the rumor about Joe?") "No, and if it's just a rumor, I guess I'd rather not hear it."

Sometimes Silence Is Insulting

Avoid: (Saying nothing as people pass by.)

Instead: "Hello (as you smile)!"

You wouldn't think universities would spend much time studying something as basic as a smile. But they have—big time. And their findings are dramatic. We seem oblivious to how significantly we're all affected by a smile, starting at ages where you wouldn't think a baby would recognize anything.

When you walk into a room smiling a warm, sincere smile and saying hello, you largely take control of that room. Conversely, when you enter a room cold and quiet, you chill the people around you.

Saying hello as you pass people is, admittedly, a cultural habit. I have lived in five different U.S. states, and they differed noticeably in how often people smiled and said hello as they walked past strangers. If you're not afraid of attracting the attention of unfamiliar people and you're not worried about having someone misconstrue your smile as flirtation, then a smile and a "good morning" is a habit worth considering. The smile-and-hello package is a powerful tool.

Example: (Smiling.) "Hello! Beautiful day."

Don't Attack People—or Places

Avoid: "I hate this place."

Instead: "We're so lucky to have this place."

Is it possible to change how much you like a place just by saying it aloud? I argue that, yes, it is. I genuinely subscribe to the Dale Carnegie notion that if you act enthusiastic, you *become* enthusiastic. The psychological framework behind such a notion is tough to pin down, but it seems to have something to do with some findings that the human brain rests on negative ideas unless positive ideas move them along (an attribute that goes back to our caveman survival days).

> **Highlight and Delete**
>
> Remember that there's a clearly defined line between attempting self-motivation and faking motivation. If people don't find your gusto legitimate, it won't catch on, and it may backfire.

So instead of being down on your old house, your job, your rotten kids, and the dog that hates you, tell yourself (and others) how lucky you are. Chances are, you're right anyway.

Example: "We're so lucky to have this place. When other businesses are crying bankruptcy or leveraging themselves right out of existence, our little shop, bought and paid for, just keeps taking care of customers and putting food on our table. We truly are blessed."

Don't Be a Negative Fortune-Teller

Avoid: "That'll *never* work."

Instead: "Sounds like a plan. What may I do to help?"

Don't spend a lot of your time negatively predicting the future. Sure, even a stopped clock tells the right time twice a day, but no one is impressed with your bleak prophecies. Besides, you can't win. If you're wrong, things are better, but your public naysaying certainly didn't help your image. If you're right, then things really are bleak and no one's happy.

If someone comes up with a reasonably sound plan and no one else has a better idea, jump on the plan with some optimism and get going. See what sort of help the planner needs. And while you're at it, thank her for the time, energy, and guts she put into the idea while everyone else was being a naysayer.

Example: "Sounds like a plan. Thanks for having the insight and energy to put it together. Does anyone have any thoughts or concerns? Any devil's-advocate apprehension? Well, let's move forward, then. What may I do to help?"

Steer Clear of Sarcasm

Avoid: "We don't need that sarcastic tone."

Instead: (Ignore the sarcasm.)

Many times, a bitter, cynical tone is meant to express exasperation, elicit an agitated response, or to accomplish both of the above.

Don't give the super-sarcastic team member what he wants, which is to distract. If he's pulling the topic off course, then he probably doesn't have much interest or ownership in what's going on anyway. Ignore the sarcasm, and it will either go away or sit there and quietly fume.

Example: (After someone says something bitter and cynical, you ignore him.) "So, any other thoughts?"

Forgo the Cheap Shot

Avoid: "You're clueless."

Instead: "Thanks for your feedback. I want to ask a few others for their input as well."

Summarily telling someone that he's amateurish or dumb might make you feel good for a split second, but it's likely that you'll feel bad later. And if you don't feel guilty, you'll certainly feel hindered; that person will never help you again and might forever be your detractor.

Instead, thank the person for his feedback, useless though it may be, and tell him that you're going to ask a few other people for their thoughts before you make any decisions. Even if he doesn't get his way, the fact that you showed the courtesy of your time and interest might make him a supporter.

Example: "Thanks for your feedback regarding the many uses of sharp, pointy objects for toddlers. Before going forward with that idea, I'm going to ask a few others for their input as well. I'll let you know how your thoughts fit in with this as soon as I can. Again, thanks."

Be the Master of Your Phone

Avoid: "Could you wait a second? My cell phone is ringing."

Instead: (Nothing. Turn your cell phone off.)

Is answering a cell phone in the middle of a conversation or important discussion the same as verbally attacking someone? I make the argument that it's just as bad, if not worse. Talking on a cell phone is akin to talking to a third, imaginary person in the room. As such, it makes the other person (the one who's really in the room) understandably uncomfortable, and maybe a bit miffed.

As I've mentioned elsewhere in this text, if you want to be a person of influence, you can't be a slave to your cell. If you're heading into a meeting or perhaps a one-on-one discussion with a boss or a colleague, you avoid suggesting to them that the phone is more important by turning it off before the conversation begins.

Admittedly, you can't stop the boss from keeping *her* phone on, and you can't give her dirty looks while she's chatting while you wait nearby. But you can observe it, note it, and say, "I'll never be that way when I'm in that position."

Example: "Beep!" (That's the sound of you turning off your cell phone before the conversation begins.)

Make 'Em Do It, but Nicely

Avoid: "You *have* to do this."

Instead: "It's important that you do this for me."

Telling someone that he *has* to do something is likely to meet with an unspoken, internal response on his part: "Oh, no I *don't*." And he might be right; he's never done it before, and yet here he is, unscathed.

Setting it in the context of a favor (even if you're in charge) puts the work directive on a much more positive track. "Hey, Ken, would you do me this favor? There are about 10 tons of defective product in the warehouse. Would you please recycle it for me?" I have watched bosses very high up constantly frame job directions as favors. Yes, everyone knows that the person, strictly speaking, can't say no. But he can sure drag his heels. Responding to a good-deed request almost invariably puts people in a more productive mood.

Example: "I know you're sick of taking charge of this annual student field trip. It means a lot to the kids and their parents, though, and you know the area better than anyone. It's important that you do this for me. Would you, please?"

The Least You Need to Know

- ◆ It is better to forget about whether you're right and the other person's wrong. Find a reasonable thread in the discussion that you *don't* disagree with and steer in that direction.

- ◆ Sincerity is exceedingly important, but a little tact goes a long way as well.

- ◆ Just as you define yourself by how you compliment people, you also define yourself by how you insult them or spread rumors about them.

- ◆ The best way to handle bitter sarcasm is to ignore it. Odds are that the sarcastic person has little vested interest in what's being discussed.

- ◆ Practice empathetic listening. It starts with turning your cell phone off.

Chapter 16

Don't Use Ten-Dollar Words

In This Chapter

- ◆ Big words with little punch
- ◆ Confusing words
- ◆ Words that mean something different
- ◆ Silly jargon
- ◆ Words that look uncomfortable

Although this isn't a vocabulary-builder text, I certainly don't have anything against vocabulary-building words. In fact, throughout this book, I've offered a few catchy-looking or catchy-sounding words. I hope you've learned a few of these new, handy words along the way.

However, knowing that gaudy doesn't necessarily mean expensive, flashy doesn't necessarily mean smart. Some big words are, well, just gaudy. Furthermore, some words look like other words, confounding many of the people who hear them or read them.

Here are some ten-dollar words that are, well, just overpriced. These words merit replacement by other words that are more straightforward and effective (and therefore more powerful).

Don't Make It Even More Confusing

Avoid: "Obfuscate."

Instead: "Confuse."

Obfuscate means to dim or to make hidden or difficult to understand. It doesn't mean "to obliterate." But that's what many people will think when they hear or read it. Others simply won't know what you're talking about. The important consideration in using any high-level word is weighing the impress factor against the confuse factor. I argue that *obfuscate* confuses a lot more than it impresses.

> **Maximizing Maxim**
>
> Dictionary author Samuel Johnson warned all the way back in the 1700s not to become awestruck by the use of big words. Suggested Johnson: "Do not accustom yourself to use big words for little matters."

And so, if you think someone's trying to confuse an issue by piling on a bunch of other agenda items, simply suggest that he's trying to "confuse the issue."

Example: "This is an important issue. Let's not confuse it by adding all these side matters to it. I urge that we keep issue as one separate agenda item."

Don't Use "Peruse"

Avoid: "Peruse."

Instead: "Examine and scrutinize."

If you ask someone to *peruse* something, there's a good chance she's going to think that you mean to casually glance at it. And in fact, she's justified in thinking that. "Casually look at" is a secondary meaning for the word *peruse*.

However, oddly, the primary meaning of the word is very different. It means to examine something in detail. So what do you do with a word when the primary and secondary meanings contradict each other? I say scrap it. Sure it sounds cool. "Would you care to *peruse* my new book?" But if the person doesn't know whether you mean skim or scrutinize, then it's not a very well-designed word, is it?

Example: "Here's the new manual. Please examine and scrutinize it over the next week, and let me know what changes you think we should make. I value your opinion on this, and I look forward to your feedback."

Don't Echo "Eco"

Avoid: "Ecologically sound." (or "Eco-friendly.")

Instead: "Environmental." (or "Environmentally friendly.")

I'm not sure when *environmental* turned into *ecological*. Maybe it was when marketers decided that "green" was the new marketing *buzzword* and that *eco-* could be placed in front of anything before selling it. I'm not badmouthing environmental ethics. But much of the stuff being portrayed as *eco-friendly* doesn't strike me as having much to do with a cleaner environment. Just because something sounds decent doesn't make it so.

If you're promoting or discussing something that's environmentally friendly, make it easy for people in the back of the room to understand what you're talking about. Say that it's "environmentally friendly." And while you're at it, make certain that it is, indeed, good for the environment.

def•i•ni•tion

A **buzzword** is a trendy word with a convincing tone. It is often a fad word within a particular marketing segment or profession. While using a buzzword may show that you are trendy, the buzzword itself may carry little meaning.

Example: "One of the best aspects of this urban development plan is its environmental features. We believe that it's possible to keep the zoning, return a large manufacturing facility to the same 10-block region, and still continue to clean up the air for all the nearby residents."

Seek Not to Recriminate

Avoid: "Recrimination."

Instead: "Counter-accusation."

Does *recrimination* mean "discrimination"? Does it have anything to do with cremation? No to both. A *recrimination* is, in fact, a revenge type of accusation, made in retaliation. Sort of like saying, "I can say meaner things than you can."

Out of all the words in this chapter, *recrimination* is probably the one I have the least beef with. After all, there's nothing wrong with making people look up a word in the dictionary every now and then. But I respectfully suggest that, if used in a meeting or in a speech, it will confuse the other people in the room. Use something like "retaliatory charge" or "counter-accusation," and people will understand exactly what you're trying to say.

Example: "It was bad enough that we had to accuse him of stealing money from the corporate coffer. But his counter-accusation of harassment has unfortunately taken this case to a whole new level."

Be Uninterested in "Disinterested"

Avoid: "Disinterested."

Instead: "Unbiased."

Disinterested, again, is one of those words whose primary and secondary definitions are so different that it's best to scrap the word altogether.

The primary definition of *disinterested* is "not interested." However, the word is used much more for its secondary definition, which is "neutral" or "unbiased." My suggestion: remove the confusion and simply say "unbiased."

Example: "What we need is an unbiased third party, such as a consultant with no ties to any of the bidders, to consider these very technical proposals and offer us some nonpolitical recommendations."

A Shorter Word—What a Concept!

Avoid: "Conceptualization."

Instead: "Concept." (or "Idea." or "Theory.")

Did you ever read the Dr. Seuss book *And to Think That I Saw It on Mulberry Street* (Vanguard Press, 1937)? The book begins with a boy watching a horse and wagon, but by the end of the story, his imagination has turned it into something of a grand parade.

My guess is that, somewhere along the way, that's what someone did with the word *concept*. It turned into *conceptual*; then to *conceptualize*; and then to *conceptualization*. But it's still just a plain horse and wagon.

Conceptualization simply means "the formation of an idea." Why not just use "idea" or "concept" instead? If you need to go a bit further, refer to the "forming of an idea."

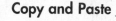

Copy and Paste

A good rule of thumb is to make sure at least 90 percent of your audience or readership understands the word you're using.

Example: "Yes, I didn't quite understand his concept at first. But after seeing the diagrams, the flow charts, and his presentation, I think I get the idea."

Don't Make It Even More Difficult

Avoid: "Arduous."

Instead: "Difficult." (or "Demanding.")

I've seen and heard the word *arduous* a lot lately. It means "difficult or demanding." The meaning, admittedly, is pretty straightforward, and the word, in and of itself, isn't too confusing or obscure.

My hang-up with *arduous* is similar to the problem with *grasping* that I mentioned in Chapter 14. That is, just as *grasping* seems perpetually connected to the word *straws, arduous* seems forever linked to *task*—an arduous task. Can there be an arduous anything else? I recommend "difficult" or "demanding" as more than worthy replacements. Besides, something can be difficult or demanding without its having to be a task.

Example: "We have presented you a very difficult task. Your team members are set in their ways. But we've watched you handle people before. You have a gift for it. And we believe you will do just fine at this demanding new post. Now go get 'em!"

Avoid the Jargon

Avoid: "Pedagogy."

Instead: "The science of teaching."

I don't like jargon. Jargon is like a hidden clubhouse with the sign "No Grown-ups Allowed" on the door. Teachers have their own little secret password into that clubhouse. It's the word *pedagogy*. No one else knows what it means. No one else cares, and rightfully so.

The problem with jargon is that it is exclusive and condescending. Why use a word that only people within one profession can understand? Is it to feel important? Is it to confuse people outside the clubhouse? I'm not sure. Psychologist Abraham Maslow's Hierarchy of Needs suggests that belongingness is a primary human need, so jargon surely serves a small purpose within a devoted professional group. That is, their language helps define them. But when people outside the group feel blocked by the jargon, then one must rightfully challenge the jargon's utility.

Highlight and Delete

The use of jargon is especially inappropriate when it makes others feel left out.

I respectfully propose that teachers the world over begin using the phrase "the science of teaching" in place of the silly, ten-dollar word *pedagogy*. We're about educating—we don't need our own playhouse.

Example: "As we examine the science of teaching, we must be certain to take into consideration an area that is too often neglected—namely, the area of adult literacy."

Be Abundantly Clear

Avoid: "Plethora."

Instead: "Overabundance."

Many people mistakenly believe that *plethora* means "plenty" or "lots." Not so, although the confusion is certainly understandable. The word *plethora*, in fact, means "too much" or "overabundance." There's a difference—a big enough difference that I recommend using "over-abundance."

As a side note, there are two words that sound enough like plethora that people only half-heartedly paying attention might think of one of them, further distracting them. Neither of these words is pleasant.

Example: "What do we do when there are more communications students in the United States than there are people working in communications? This overabundance of media students suggests that colleges should steer their majors more toward employer needs than students' wistful desires."

Don't Overuse "Community"

Avoid: "I admire his sense of community."

Instead: "I admire how he cares for his neighbors."

Community seems an odd choice for this chapter, but I argue that the phrase "sense of community" has been overused recently. That, in and of itself, isn't so bad—except that it doesn't mean a darned thing. "Sense of community" is one of those empty phrases that people feel comfortable using as a compliment but, when filleted, really doesn't seem to have any meat to it.

If someone really *does* care for his neighbors, just say he does.

Example: "He's a strong politician. But he's also a good person. I admire how he cares for his neighbors by following up on odd requests or checking up on mundane things such as garbage pickup and street-sweeping schedules."

Use Spectacular Vernacular

Avoid: "Vernacular."

Instead: "Conversational speech."

Can you hear or see *vernacular* without thinking "spectacular"? If so, you're a better person than I am. *Vernacular* is one of those words that seems to be used by many people but not entirely understood by most of them.

Vernacular, simply put, means "conversational speech"—specifically, the conversational speech of a particular region. I recommend the phrase "conversational speech."

Example: "If one is going to delve deeply into a culture, he or she needs to study its culture, its value system, and its conversational speech."

The Least You Need to Know

♦ Just because a word looks or sounds flashy doesn't mean it's valuable to your speech or to your essay. Often, the more straightforward and effective a word is, the more powerful it is.

♦ Some big words are detrimental because their primary and secondary meanings seem to contradict each other.

♦ Some big words are unfavorable because they look or sound like other words with very different meanings.

♦ If jargon promotes a sense of belonging within a tight-knit, professional group, it might have a small purpose. But if it becomes condescending or obstructive to people outside the group, avoid it.

5

Mind Tricks That Aren't (Too) Evil

No one wants to be the victim of a mind trick. We all tend to consider our own minds as sacred territory, not to be toyed with or manipulated. And you'll surely be ostracized if you're caught trying to mess with *someone else's* mind.

However, there are a few effective strategies that involve words that are innocent. These strategies involve little more than structuring a phrase, sentence, or compliment properly. But they do offer enough of a positive side effect or subliminal message as to fall into the "suggestive" category.

Project the good thoughts you have for others back on yourself. Do this by using hidden mechanisms within words and—when the situation allows it—by creating new words that function better than any existing ones.

Chapter 17

Compliment Away! (It'll Come Right Back to You)

In This Chapter

- What goes around comes around
- Syrupy and grateful
- Compliments with details
- Thanks and appreciation
- A question as a compliment

An interesting psychosocial study not too long ago discovered that when you say something nice about a person who's not around, the people in the room subliminally relate the compliment to *you* along with the person you're saying it about! So why not say nice things about people all day long, if it means saying things (humbly) about yourself?

Granted, no one likes a phony, and the admiring comments should be sincere. But if you take the time to pay tribute to the hard work and pleasant attitude of others, it's good to know that, compliment-wise, what goes around comes around. Here are some effective ways to compliment others. It makes everyone feel good: the people who hear the compliment (because they know it might be one of them next time), the person being complimented (because he or she appreciates the public nod of approval), and you (because it feels good saying nice things and you know the good thoughts will be projected back on you).

People Remember the Nice Things You Say

Weak: "Jim does okay work."

Powerful: "Jim is a hard worker and a great problem solver."

If you say pleasant things about other people, a healthy, potent aura of good feelings surrounds you. You instantly become associated with the kind appraisals that you offer. If you're sincere about someone's noteworthy effort, that sincerity will ring true in your words.

And if someone's work is acceptable or just okay, why not spice up your observation a bit? Pay him a compliment that he might try to live up to. Whether you deliver the compliment straight to the person or pass it through other friends or colleagues, your compliment may pose a challenge. And because the challenge was made in the form of a compliment, the person just might strive for a higher standard. However things turn out, people will remember you as a person who says nice things. And that's a good thing.

Example: "Jim is a hard worker and a great problem solver. He is very dependable. We'll have to make a point of thanking him for this latest production record."

Compliment the Expertise

Weak: "You've got to admit this is a bad idea."

Powerful: "You're the experienced mind in this area, and your knowledge is expert and hands-on. Aren't you a little concerned that perhaps this is a bad idea?"

If you're trying to sway someone in a particular direction, it's not too corny to do so with a compliment and a question. In this case the compliment works best when it's tied to something the person seems to know very well. "Hey Roy, you know marketing better than anyone. Don't you think this complimentary paper hat is the way to go?"

Again, don't be phony or empty in your complimenting. Offer a compliment that's fitting and sincere. But if you tender it before asking a persuasion-driven question, it will set up the conversation on a much more pleasant note.

Example: "You're the experienced mind regarding computer network distribution, and clearly your knowledge is expert and hands-on. Aren't you a little concerned that perhaps this new operating system is a bad idea?"

Be Syrupy Sometimes

Weak: "Can you help me?"

Powerful: "I heard that the best-looking/smartest/kindest person around today was in this area, and so I thought I'd find you and ask for your help."

Not too long ago, the rock group Bon Jovi was offering a free concert in Central Park in New York City. However, the concert was to be fenced off, and would-be concertgoers had to put their names into a lottery. The prospects weren't good for my wife and her sister, two big Bon Jovi fans.

A few days before the big concert, at a July 4th celebration, rumors were floating around that workers from the city's vintage rock station were randomly handing out tickets. I said to my wife, "Watch the master at work."

I walked up to two young ladies wearing the rock station's employee shirt. "Excuse me," I said. "Could you help me? I heard that the two most attractive young ladies in the park were handing out Bon Jovi tickets. It appears that you're they, and so I thought I should ask you if it were true."

> **Maximizing Maxim** _____
>
> Is it possible to make someone feel obligated to you just because you paid him or her a compliment? In the 1920s, French sociologist Marcel Mauss offered just such an argument. In his work *The Gift* (Routledge, 1990), Mauss suggested that giving someone either a gift or a compliment created a sort of dominance over that other person. Argued Mauss: "The gift not yet repaid debases the man who accepts it."

They looked at each other as if to say, "Oh brother, what a line!" But it worked. One of them pulled out two tickets, handed them to me, and I returned to my wife, her mouth hanging open in disbelief. She and her sister enjoyed the show a few nights later.

Just because it's corny, and *you* know it's corny, and the *other* person knows it's corny, doesn't mean you can't sometimes say it. I'll walk into my home, see my wife, and say, "Wait a moment." I'll leave and immediately re-enter the house. "It's true. You *are* better-looking each time I see you!" Yes, it's syrupy and dumb. But my wife knows that, beneath the corn, I really do find her beautiful.

Example: "Hello. I heard that the smartest librarian in the state was working here today, and so I thought I'd find you and ask for your help. Would you happen to have any paper publications on American gender issues of the early 1800s?"

Show Gratitude and Express Appreciation

Weak: (Saying nothing.)

Powerful: "Thank you." (or "Thank you. I appreciate your help.")

We already talked in Chapters 3, 8, and 12 about expressing thanks. If it made good book-writing sense, I would repeat those sections here verbatim. I cannot overemphasize the importance of saying "thank you" or "I appreciate your effort." And just as making compliments makes you look and feel good, so does expressing thanks and appreciation.

You may say it, or you may write it down, but whatever you do, act on the impulse and express it. There's no one more unpleasant to be around than someone who feels undervalued or underappreciated.

Haven't we all been there?—"Why should I bother to do my best work if no one is going to notice anyway?" But if Bob in the mail room or Sue in the marketing department *knows* that someone is going to notice, and that someone is going to appreciate his or her effort, then Bob and Sue might just put forth some *extra* effort. Maybe they'll do their jobs a little better. They'll feel good. And they'll feel good about *you* because you noticed, and you said so.

Example: (Written on a nice piece of stationery because your thanks are so sincere—and important.) Thank you for your help on this project, Brad. Your sense of humor brought welcome relief on those tight deadline days. And your reworking of the employee bonus policy was masterful.

Use "Because"

Weak: "Your tie looks nice."

Powerful: "Your tie looks nice because it goes so well with your jacket."

It sounds like a lot of work, but if you're going to offer sincere compliments that have impact, you should get into specifics. Don't worry, the other person won't mind. She'll appreciate that someone cared enough to notice.

An example would be paying attention to someone's new neck scarf at work. Instead of simply saying, "I like your scarf," you add a detail or two. "I like your new scarf." Maybe a bit more: "I like the pattern on your new scarf."

And then, just when you feel like you've gone far enough, you give him a *because* as to *why* you like the scarf. "Hey, I really like the pattern on that new scarf because it goes perfectly with the jacket you're wearing." Guess what? That's what *he* had thought in the store, and that's why he had purchased it the night before.

Highlight and Delete

Gauge your workplace before paying compliments regarding looks, clothing, or weight loss. Some highly charged work environments consider most flattering remarks about physical attributes or grooming to be inappropriate.

When admiring someone's clothing, you don't have to limit yourself to colors and patterns. You might comment on how a shirt brings out the color in someone's eyes. You might comment on how well a new coat hangs on a person. You might compliment the nice tailoring of a new suit. The important thing is that it looks good to you and that you're sincere with your accolade.

So remember, compliment the article of clothing and, using the word *because*, tell him why it looks especially good on him. He will appreciate the compliment as well as the detailed supporting comments. You will have made someone feel good about shopping and dressing up a bit.

This method of complimenting need not be limited to cosmetics. Consider the impact of this compliment when delivered to a colleague: "I appreciate the presentation you gave in the meeting this morning because it was well organized and succinct. An excellent summary of our third-quarter activity."

Example: "I like the pattern on your new tie because it goes well with that tweed jacket. Very nice combination. You look quite distinguished today!"

Give a Little Credit

Weak: "They really screwed *that* up."

Powerful: "I really give them credit for tackling an especially tough job."

As mentioned in Chapter 15, several studies recently suggested that the human mind locks in on negative thoughts when positive thoughts aren't proactively coaxing it along. It's an inherent characteristic that's traced back to our early days as survivalists. The bottom line is that your mind automatically goes back to negativity unless you stay positive.

There's probably something constructive and encouraging to be drawn from just about any experience, even the truly bad ones at work. Failure stifles many people. The upbeat person, however, addresses the disappointment, tries to learn from it, looks at whatever bright side there might be (a thousand years from now, who's gonna care?), and moves on.

Perhaps that's why people who regularly try but fail still deserve our recognition. They're failing because they're trying. At the very least, no one has to stop by and brush the dust off of them. And as with spaghetti thrown against a wall, one of these days, something's going to stick for those people. Maybe they'll remember how encouraging and complimentary you were when things were low. Maybe they'll take you around in their limo!

If you want to know the best direction to channel your power words and compliments, it's toward the person who keeps trying to find a solution when everyone else has given up. That's someone who deserves a rave review.

Example: "Well, things didn't turn out exactly as planned. But I really give those folks credit for tackling an especially tough job."

Ask a Question

Weak: "It looks like you know what you're doing."

Powerful: "How did you do that?"

Many of the great motivation experts, including the late, great master Dale Carnegie, have maintained that one of the best ways to hold positive influence over someone is to get him talking about himself. And so, this book continues its chaotic swing between panning the self-serving nature of people and accepting it and working with it in our quest for power through words.

Here's another great way to spread icing on the cake of a compliment. Follow the praise immediately with a question about how the person managed to do whatever it is you've just complimented. "Man oh man, you always seem to bring the best-waxed car into the parking lot. I could shave in that mirrored shine! How do you get a car looking like that?" Assuming the person is passionate about good paint jobs and good wax jobs, he'll probably tell you all about it proud as can be throughout the discussion.

It's not really 100 percent self-importance that makes people enjoy talking about their passions. Sure, vanity has something to do with it. But it's also just as likely that because compliments are so rare these days, people claw onto them when they occur. Also, because no one seems to listen anymore, an interested ear is also a nice surprise. When was the last time someone asked *you* about *your* life passion and listened keenly as you told him about it?

Example: "Boy, that was really a long drive, and right down the middle of the fairway! How did you do that?"

Say It in Front of Others

Weak: "Congratulations." (in private)

Powerful: "Congratulations." (in front of peers)

Recognition in front of one's peers is really a pleasure to watch and be a part of, even if you're not the one receiving the tribute. A person might resist, say he won't attend, or hide his face when the camera begins flashing. But more often than not, when he stands up to accept this mark of respect, he's full of pride and delighted to be on hand.

If you really want to show off this person's accomplishments, invite someone from a level or two up the company to attend. Hmmm, you'll be there while the big boss is there. Did you plan it that way? Maybe so, but it's still all about the person who's receiving the congratulations. If one of your team members is receiving an award, you should make a point to be on hand and be visible. He's your teammate—enjoy a small bit of boss-related recognition.

Example: "I wanted to take this opportunity at our department lunch today to congratulate Jim for his recent award from the Alliance of Gastrointestinal Endoscopic Surgeons. His tireless work in developing new scopes with clearer images makes this award very, very appropriate. Well done, Jim." (Applause.)

Display Your Confidence in Them (and in Yourself)

Weak: "Ah, give it a shot."

Powerful: "I know you can do it."

"Well, do your best, and let's see what happens." Yikes! There's not much confidence in that line, is there? If a person has the basic knowledge to get a task done and he's excited about making it happen, how about a little encouragement? "I've seen you do this before, albeit on a small scale. I'll be with you every step of the way. I know you can do it." Say it confidently, mentor the person, and watch him surprise everyone by kicking butt.

People very often rise to the level of challenge and responsibility that they're given. That is, they grow into a role that, earlier, may have seemed too much for them to handle. Allow people the opportunity to grow into a compliment, challenge, or task. That's not being overly optimistic; it's allowing yourself to be surprised, in a good way, by people you know, time and time again.

One quick advertisement: this one's for integrity. If someone doesn't have the most basic skills or knowledge to get a task done, don't suggest that she does. There's a difference between rising to a challenge and magically waking up one morning with a machine operator's license that she never trained or tested for.

One more quick advertisement: this one's for the self-confidence involved in showing confidence in others. Just as compliments reflect on you, so does the confidence you show to others. It takes a lot of confidence in oneself to express and display an appropriate amount of confidence in others. The delightful news is that, once you display the right dose of confidence in others—to the point at which they ace a particular task—your confidence in yourself will also increase considerably.

Example: "I've watched you do some amazing things over the years. This new challenge is just one more way for you to show the world what you're made of. I know you can do it."

The Least You Need to Know

◆ When you deliver compliments, the people in the room subliminally relate the compliment to you along with the person you're saying it about.

◆ Offering a compliment before making a request, if done sincerely, sets up the request on a much more pleasant note.

◆ You make yourself very special when you thank people or express appreciation, especially when you write your thoughts in a hand-written note.

◆ When complimenting someone, add *because*, as in, "You do a nice job because you're so consistent." Convey a compliment with a question, such as, "How do you manage to balance so many tasks at once?"

◆ The impact of a compliment increases dramatically when it is delivered in the presence of the person's colleagues.

Chapter 18

Send Subliminal Messages

In This Chapter

- ◆ Pleasant sounds
- ◆ Hidden meanings
- ◆ Expert and peer opinion
- ◆ Word games
- ◆ Using sex to sell

If a movie theater flashes the words *EAT POPCORN* for a thousandth of a second in the middle of a movie, are you more inclined—though mentally oblivious to what you've just seen—to leave for the snack line? What about words cleverly buried in the soundtrack of a commercial? When you hear these words subconsciously, are you more likely to run out for a burger?

In fact, much of what we think we know about subliminal perception is largely unproven. While the notion of mind control through music and pictures is fascinating, studies involving mind stimuli just below our threshold of awareness are largely inconclusive.

There are, however, several effective hidden devices within words. They're not subliminal in the sense that they don't consciously register: we clearly hear the words being said. The subliminal nature of these words is that their purposes are often concealed—and yet these purposes are often effective.

So consider the word-mind tricks mentioned next. You might decide, guilt-free, to use them. (None of them is unethical.) Or you might catch other people using them and refuse to be fooled.

Use Words You Want Attached to You

Weak: "Andy's smart, but not as smart as I am."

Powerful: "Andy's smart. Man, that Andy is one smart guy. Boy, is he *smart*."

Remember how we said in Chapter 17 that the nice things you say tend to attach themselves to you, even though you're saying the nice things about other people? Well, the same is true of the not-so-nice things you say. People tend to relate the sharp words just as much with you as with the person you're condemning.

Copy and Paste

Make sure that all of your compliments are sincere. Sincerity is the grease that keeps the engine of persuasion running.

The studies that back up this concept don't dwell on karma or people benefitting from their own good ways. The findings are much more psychology-based; people have a propensity to remember your name and face with adjectives you've used to describe other people. So, watch what you say about others.

Unfortunately, this trick doesn't work with physical attributes. I've been commenting on how tall other people are for years, but it hasn't added 1 cm to my height!

Example: "That Kenny's smart. He never ceases to amaze me with his gift for analyzing difficult choices and selecting the wisest path. He's a real sharp guy."

Sow Consent

Weak: "Do you …?"

Powerful: "To what extent do you …?"

As mentioned in Chapter 2, sometimes one of the most efficient ways to begin a proposal is to introduce it as if you have complete consent. Tell people about the program as if they've already said yes to it. Tell what it will do for them, how much it costs, and what else it will entail from them. Talk about it in light of how amazing this plan is and how everyone else must already be thinking *yes, yes, yes!*

Salespeople are especially good with this tactic; it's their bread and butter. "So, would you like to leave today with the coupe or the sedan?" "Do you prefer the silver one or the red one?" "Are you interested in a three-year or five-year loan?" "Do you have a trade-in?" Nowhere in his banter will you hear, "So, kind sir, will you consider purchasing a car from me today?"

Yes, the confident person (like you) may respond with, "I haven't made up my mind yet." But there are a lot of unconfident people out there who are more than willing to allow the powerful person to show them the way. Plus, if you assume consent from the start, even with equally confident people, you plant encouraging seeds of suggestion.

Example: "So that's the plan, Joe. To what extent do you see your department contributing to this effort?"

Use a Rhetorical Question as a Compliment

Weak: "You are a very charitable person."

Powerful: "Really, is there anyone more charitable than you?"

People have a tough time accepting a compliment. They say things such as, "It's no big deal," or "Oh, this old thing?" And so, offering well-deserved (and inspiring) compliments becomes awkward for both parties. And most times, we tend to avoid giving them. Life would be so much easier if someone said to you, "What a nice sweater that is," and you responded with, "Why, thank you."

> **Copy and Paste** _____
>
> You will have a much easier time offering compliments if you can get into the groove of accepting them. The next time someone offers you a compliment, don't humble yourself by saying, "Oh, it was nothing." Instead, offer the compliment the hardy, "Why, thank you," that it deserves.

But just because compliments are sometimes tough to offer doesn't mean you should avoid making them. Receiving compliments is much too mentally stimulating for influential people to ignore. The key is to submit an admiring comment in a way that is pleasant for both parties.

I like word expert Samara O'Shea's solution to the awkward compliment conundrum. In her book *For the Love of Letters* (HarperCollins, 2007), she suggests offering a compliment as a rhetorical question. In other words, she recommends that you offer a compliment in the form of a question that's meant more as a statement than a request for information. "Wow, Nathan, is there anyone better dressed than you?" Or perhaps, "Wow, Katie, is there anyone better at selecting good metal music than you?" The person might casually respond, "I'm sure there are" as some sort of reflex. And at that point, the compliment has already been delivered, and in comfortable fashion for both parties.

Example: "Really, Mary-Jane, is there anyone more kind and caring than you?"

Mention the Big Kahuna

Weak: "I thought it important to show this to you."

Powerful: "Mr. Boss asked me to show this to you."

If you're trying to persuade someone to listen to your pitch, dropping an important name is likely to help.

I'm not suggesting this method for approaching someone within your organization. However, if you're approaching someone at another company and you mention that the big boss heard about your plan and liked it, then you're likely to have the attention of those you approach.

Getting things approved when you're not part of the organization doesn't have to follow a perfect chain of command up or down.

If you can't reach the big boss, talk to an administrative assistant and make a quick pitch. If the assistant refers you to someone lower, follow up and mention the assistant's name; the administrative assistants or secretaries of the big bosses hold a lot more sway than you might think.

Example: "Mr. Bigboss asked me to show this to you. It's a new plan for placing one of our small refrigerators in each employee's cubicle. He felt that it would keep people at their desks, being productive, for longer periods of time. The fridges are inexpensive and, without freezers, are energy efficient. Your employees will love it!"

Be Milgram

Weak: "Would you please finish this task?"

Powerful: "You must continue."

In the 1960s, Yale psychologist Stanley Milgram scared a lot of people by showing how easily human beings could be ordered to do just about anything. In the experiment, the people were asked to administer electric shocks in a faux learning experiment. (The shocks, too, were faked.) The vast majority of people administering the shocks continued to do so even when they thought the voltage levels were harmful or deadly. Milgram's findings were unsettling in that it made us consider the possibility that we're hardwired for obeying authority.

Incidentally, Milgram later on was criticized for putting his subjects through the anxiety of such an experiment. Said Milgram: "I'm convinced that much of the criticism, whether people know it or not, stems from the results of the experiment. If everyone had broken off at slight shock or moderate shock, this would be a very reassuring finding, and who would protest?"

Without delving into the psychology of it, know that when something is necessary or urgent, most people will do what they're told by an authority figure, though they might complain or protest.

Example: (After someone says, "Can't I put this off for some other time? It doesn't seem all that important.") "You must continue."

Belittle with Quotation Marks

Weak: "He's a commercial writer in the city."

Powerful: "He's a 'commercial writer' in the city."

Just about everything in this book is positive in nature because being influential generally means being positive. However, there are those occasions in which you might need to take a gentle swipe at someone without seeming too mean-spirited. For example, if you believe someone is lying but the situation merits a dose of discretion, then a small dig might be the order of the day.

My favorite swat is, when writing about something I've heard that I don't agree with, to place the item in quotation marks. Yes, the contractor claims the building will be done "in two years." Rather than calling the promise bogus or wildly optimistic, I simply place it in quotation marks, as if to say, "Those are his silly words—not mine."

If you want to be a lot more obvious and biting, you might try the word *so-called* or the word *alleged*. "That so-called consultant says he can reduce our costs by half." "The project allegedly will be completed by the spring." Be careful. If the person you're talking about reads or hears these words, he'll know you're insulting him. With the quotation marks, it's not quite so clear—or blatant.

Highlight and Delete

> Don't write or say anything that you wouldn't want everyone you know to read or hear. With electronic communication and sound reproduction these days, it is very easy to find a private e-mail or a hush-hush meeting surprisingly transmitted to all.

This indirect message is only for writing. I don't suggest you become like the late comedian Chris Farley's character, Matt Foley, with his quotation-mark fingers violently bobbing up and down.

Example: "My future son-in-law calls himself 'an independent contractor.'"

Make 'Em Professional

Weak: "He's a musician."

Powerful: "He's a professional musician."

In contrast to the previous item, I suggest you use the word *professional* (without the quotation marks) whenever you want to enrich a person's job title or proposal. For example, if you call someone an actor, often the implication is that he's mostly waiting on tables. But if you write or say that he's a professional actor, then the upbeat implication is that he's making something of a living as an actor.

Apply this concept to a colleague. Suppose someone's about to present to a roomful of people a project proposal or some sort of formal recommendation. You can introduce the person and "his professional proposal." Again, the positive implication is that he's paid to know what he's doing, and that he does a good job at making and implementing recommendations.

Maximizing Maxim

What's in a job title? Lots. Some studies suggest that most people are inclined to select a more motivational-sounding job title over one that pays more. iVillage UK career editor Irene Krechowiecka suggests that if you like your position title, you're more likely to work harder. She notes: "As well as affecting motivation, an inspiring job title can increase your confidence." Her suggestion if you don't care for your title: approach your boss about having it changed, especially during a performance review.

Example: "Peter is a very professional furniture arranger. He has put together a proposal for arranging our new office. Let's give him the courtesy of listening to his professional presentation."

Everyone's Doin' It

Weak: "Are you going to scrub that floor?"

Powerful: "Are you going to join us for the annual Floor Scrub Party?"

Not too long ago, one of the bosses in my building ordered a bunch of assembly-required tables. Those tables sat there, packed in cardboard boxes, for the entire summer. People routinely walked past them, commenting to each other, "Darned if *I'm* going to help put those things together." I admit, I thought the same way: I was much too important a person to assemble furniture.

Finally, just before the point at which these tables were needed, this boss went into the room with lots of food and some good music playing on the boom box, and she began to assemble 20 tables herself.

Of course, you've read the rest of the story in Mark Twain's *Tom Sawyer* (American Publishing Company, 1884). It didn't look too tough, and she seemed to be having a fun, productive time. Before an hour had passed, the room was filled with colleagues eating food, joking, and putting together those tables. The job was completed in less than three hours. (Hey, is it my imagination, or did she *leave* at some point, allowing us to finish ourselves? Clever gal.)

It's not so much peer pressure as it is the pleasure of feeling as if one belongs to a group. Tap into that feeling whenever you have to dish out tough work. "Would you care to join us for our annual Spring Cleaning Extravaganza? Music, food, fun. You're welcome to join us." The appealing part of this gimmick is that, in the end, the difficult work *will* wind up being fun (or at least tolerable). You will have made it so.

Example: "Hi, Kitty. Are you going to join us for our conference room painting party? A fun time is guaranteed for all. We'll be calling for carryout. The boom box will be on the local oldies station. Interested?"

Repeat a Letter

Weak: "I didn't trust him when he entered the room."

Powerful: "He slithered along the stairway and into my space, and I instantly spotted his sneaky style."

Alliteration is one of those crafty literary devices that we often read, are affected by, but to which we are oblivious. Alliteration is the repeating of the same letter at the beginning of several different words. "The complete idiot courageously acquired this comprehensive copy."

By repeating the *m* sound, you might create a hidden humming or moaning within a sentence. By repeating the *s* sound, you might insinuate a slyness that's taking place. By repeating the *t* sound, you might hint at a certain preciseness or punctuality.

Example: "When it's the voters versus the vermin of corruption, it's the voters who come out valiant and victorious."

Jab with a Dysphemism

Weak: "He just arrived with his assistants."

Powerful: "He just arrived with his groupies."

Whereas a *euphemism* is a nice way of saying something that otherwise would have been unpleasant, a *dysphemism* is a way of making something, good or bad, sound worse than it is. For example, referring to a part-time security guard as a "rent-a-cop" would be a dysphemism.

def•i•ni•tion

A **euphemism** is a mild replacement for an offensive expression. For example, "eccentric" is a euphemism for "crazy."

Conversely, a **dysphemism** is an (often mildly) impolite word or expression used in place of a more neutral one. For example, calling a spokesman a "mouthpiece" is a dysphemism.

The cool thing about dysphemisms is that, similar to using quotation marks or alliteration, they don't have to be openly demeaning. Calling a long-term elected official "a career politician" might be meant as a jab, but then again, it might not. Your degree of debasing is to your choosing, from slight all the way up to blasphemy.

Example: "He's a legend in his own mind."

Relate It to Sex

Weak: "A room full of attractive people."

Powerful: "A sexually charged room."

If your audience is adult and mature, you might want to rely on that old standby—sex. Some advertisers will tell you that sex isn't everything: it's the *only* thing! I don't know that I agree, but I do believe that our intrinsic tendency toward procreation makes most of us highly responsive to the thought or the mention of sex, even if unconsciously so.

Of course, I'm not talking about images of writhing bodies on piles of velvet. After all, political correctness is often the order of the day. But there are ways to introduce sex or sexuality into any sort of write-up or proposal without being obvious or offensive.

For example, if you'd like to catch the immediate attention of an audience, you might introduce "these naked facts." If you want your company to consider a new logo, you might allude to its "curvaceous design and desirable colors." Nothing dirty about that, right? But the innuendo is unquestionably there.

Example: "We believe that our customers' attraction to this new product line will be visceral, instinctive, and animal-like."

The Least You Need to Know

◆ Although the effectiveness of subliminal messages embedded in movies, photos, and songs is scientifically arguable, there are several strategies of word usage that are genuinely effective, even on a subconscious level.

◆ People instinctively respond positively to references of authority and peer approval because they like the sound of positive comments—wherever these comments are pointed.

◆ You can covertly make something sound more important by adding the word *professional* (sans quotation marks) or less noteworthy by adding quotation marks to imply the word *alleged*. You can also diminish something by using a lesser word to describe it without openly seeming to put it down.

◆ You can add a certain mood to a sentence by repeating a particular letter over and over again.

◆ For adult audiences or readership, working mild, almost unnoticeable sexual innuendo into your written or spoken words will increase the attention these words garner.

Chapter 19

Create New Words

In This Chapter

◆ Adding letters

◆ Combining and flipping words

◆ Using nouns as adjectives

◆ From purpose to name

◆ From non-English to English

If you can't find the right word, you can always make up a new one. I'm not talking about those clever websites where you register a new, cute word to describe dimples on a dog. I'm talking about legitimate words that serve a purpose and might, at some point, make their way into common use.

Some years ago, I was writing a serious academic essay about the possibility of U.S. colleges becoming so alike that their programs, reputations, and tuitions would all gravitate toward sameness. That is, college education might become something of a commodity—a common good sold at the lowest price. I couldn't find the proper term for the concept, and so I created my own: the commodification of higher education. "You'll never get away with it," challenged a colleague of mine.

But I did. In fact, I used the term throughout my doctoral dissertation, and I've since employed it in several essays. If a word does the trick, even the stuffiest academic types will let it go. Better still, if the word serves a grand purpose and you're the only one using it for the time being, you're all the more commanding with your words.

Use a *Y*

Weak: "The air was fresh, and it smelled like melons."

Powerful: "The air was fresh and *melon-y*."

The words *roomy*, *dreamy*, and *leafy* didn't just come into existence. Some brainy person saw a word, saw a need, and added a *y*. And I would imagine he or she had a fun time making it up. Unless you're writing a very formal report, you may add a *y* to most any noun to create an adjective. Have fun! Be clever! Be creative!

Some minor barriers: if a word ends with a long *e* or a long *i* sound, then adding a *y* might be clunky, especially if it's a word you plan on reading aloud. For example, if you want to describe a piece of country property as "tree-y," you might have a tough time saying that one or, at any rate, relaying the meaning. Also, be cognizant of the names of the people receiving your report. A few of their names might end in a *y* sound, and the overlapping might be awkward. For example, if you describe a melon-y smelling room, Melanie might be uncomfortable with your description.

Example: "Decorated for fall, the room was all orange and pumpkiny."

Use a Hyphen

Weak: "I own a company that streamlines people's payroll operations and makes them more efficient."

Powerful: "I run a *simplified-payroll* company."

I love hyphens. I use them like crazy. A hyphen can streamline a description, meaning that you are able to get your point across quickly before you lose someone's attention. For example, if you describe a vase as a little bit orange and a little bit yellow, you've taken way too much time. But if you refer to the yellow-orange vase, then you've used a hyphen effectively.

> ### Maximizing Maxim
>
> Make sure that your newly created words serve more purpose than simply to show how clever you are. Using words simply for the sake of sounding smart won't do you much good. Two U.S. presidents saw right through such folly. Abraham Lincoln, commenting on a fellow lawyer, once said, "He can compress the most words into the small ideas better than any man I ever met." Dwight D. Eisenhower once quipped, "An intellectual is a man who takes more words than necessary to tell more than he knows!"

I especially like marketing expert Barry Callen's many uses for hyphens. In his great book *Perfect Phrases for Sales and Marketing Copy* (McGraw-Hill, 2008), Callen suggests using a hyphen to combine what services you provide with the benefit your particular services bring to people. For example, you could say that you run a drive-thru-haircut service. The service is the haircut. The benefit is that it's drive-thru and, hence, very convenient. When people ask you what you do for a living, instead of blathering on and losing their interest, you say, "I run a drive-thru-haircut service." Boom! With one three-part hyphenated word, you've gotten their interest (and, hopefully, their business).

Example: "I'm a power-book writer."

Describe the Maniac

Weak: "She's always on her cell phone."

Powerful: "She's a *cell-phone-iac*."

Combining the word *maniac* with another word works nicely, especially when the other word ends with an *n* sound. Do you love visiting Spokane? Then perhaps you're a Spokaniac. Do you go crazy whenever Dean Martin is on the radio? Then maybe you're a Dean Martiniac (pronounced *Mar-TIN-ee-ack*). Sounds like martini, doesn't it? Hmmm. The gimmick works as well with one-syllable words of all kinds. For example, if you love the taste of mints, you might be a mintiac. If you love collecting vintage baseball cards, you might be a baseball cardiac. Just don't get caught stealing those cards: you could end up under cardiac arrest!

If you use this device with a word that ends with an *e* sound, add a hyphen and the letters *ack*. Are you obsessed with the smell of strawberries? Perhaps you're a strawberry-ack. Can't get enough of Britney Spears's new CD? You must be a Britney-ack. Did I just watch you eat an entire box of chocolate cookies? Perhaps you're a certifiable chocolate cookie-ack. Again, this particular method is meant to be fun and to make your words interesting to others.

Example: "As a Jersey girl, she's a bona fide Bruce Springsteeniac."

Turn a Celebrity into an Adjective

Weak: "Well, how very mysterious!"

Powerful: "Well, how very *Mary Higgins Clark!*"

Okay, so my writing's not the greatest. But please don't get all George Plimpton on me.

Did you laugh? If you did, then perhaps you knew that the late George Plimpton was a famous writer and actor, with a well-known snobbish persona that hid his down-to-earth love for baseball and fireworks.

Turning nouns—especially people's names—into adjectives might not get you a good grade in English class, but if it's done well, it will get the attention of those listening to you or reading your correspondence. You can either add the word *like* to the person ("He had an Elvislike presence when he entered the room") or you can simply use the name in front of the noun you're describing ("Her Marilyn Monroe giggle was appealing").

Highlight and Delete

Don't use a celebrity as a common reference if you're unsure how much of a celebrity he or she is. For example, if your readership is international, don't use a celebrity unknown outside the United States as a reference for characteristics, mannerisms, or modifiers.

Depending on the audience or readership, you might make the reference very obvious or rather obscure. In front of an audience, you might say, "The Ronald Reagan nature of his patriotism is inspiring." On paper, you might write, "He has a John Nance Garner air of celebrity." If someone looks up the reference, he will find that Garner was one of Franklin D. Roosevelt's vice presidents, and that Garner spent much of his tenure hidden and a bit tipsy. Whether obvious or obscure, make the allusion fun and witty.

Example: "My wife and I have your typical Ozzie and Harriet marriage."

Turn a Movie into an Adjective

Weak: "He came back unexpectedly and stronger."

Powerful: "He pulled a *Terminator* on us."

While you're busy turning celebrities' names into adjectives, why not try the same with movie titles? "I had *Silence of the Lambs* chills come over me." "She has a *Back to the Future* kind of wholesomeness."

Again, if you want an instant response while you're giving a speech, you might make the movie reference obvious. If you're writing an essay that's going to be read by, say, talent agents, you might make the reference relatively obscure so that your readership will get the clever allusion as if it were a secret code. And if they don't get it, they might have some fun looking it up. "Yeah, their *Night of the Comet* enthusiasm is hard to turn off." *Night of the Comet* was a low-budget but very cool 1980s horror film starring Catherine Mary Stewart as a Valley girl and Kelli Maroney as her cheerleading kid sister. Since Maroney was also a cheerleader in *Fast Times at Ridgemont High*, you could also use her name as a relatively obscure celebrity reference: "Her Kelli Maroney enthusiasm is hard to turn off."

Copy and Paste

If you use a movie as a reference point in a speech, give the audience a moment to make the connection. You don't want to make an important point while they're thinking about an entertaining movie you just mentioned.

Example: "Their secret, *Casablanca* love ended sadly."

Create a Portmanteau

Weak: "He has attractive American and Asian features."

Powerful: "He has attractive *Amerasian* features."

Just as a portmanteau is a two-compartment suitcase, a *portmanteau word* is the merging of two words and their meanings. For example, *breakfast* and *lunch* merge for *brunch*, a meal that falls between breakfast and lunch and has food offerings from both. I have lots of favorite portmanteaus. Toward the top of my list is *Bennifer*, used to describe the tabloid hype surrounding Ben Affleck and Jennifer Lopez back when they were dating. I also like *cybrarian* for a cyber, or Internet, librarian. My least favorite? It's perhaps everyone's least favorite—a *spork*, that plastic hybrid of a spoon and a fork. The word is just as ugly as the device.

def•i•ni•tion

A **portmanteau word** is a word formed by combining the parts of two other words. Usually, the new word also merges elements of the original words' two meanings. Example: teleconference.

Be a little careful with these types of combinations: sometimes they have a tendency to become either clichéd and/or politically incorrect. For example, the term *Afro-American* has been wholly inappropriate since the 1980s, and I'm guessing *homoeroticism* and *Spanglish* aren't far behind.

Example: "He's made lots of money as a dentist over the years. These days, managing 10 offices, he's a regular *drillionaire*."

I Have *Ize* for You

Weak: "The sunlamp makes the shorter, winter days seem more like summer."

Powerful: "The sunlamp *summerizes* the shorter, winter days.

Placing *ize* at the end of many nouns creates clever, easy-to-comprehend verbs. These words carry very little possibility of being clichéd or culturally exiled, and they may be used in just about any written or spoken venue. And, best of all, they are easy to come up with.

Are you about to add extra insulation to your windows for the tough winter ahead? Then you're about to *weatherize* your home. Did you make some filing and ergonomic changes at the office to make things more productive? Then perhaps you *productivized* your work environment.

Note that this technique doesn't work very well with words that end in vowel sounds. For example, if you change a standard procedure at work to reflect an eight-hour daily schedule, you can't really say that you *dailyized* the rule. If you paint a mural in your home with your favorite prayer, you can't really say that you *prayized* the wall.

But often, adding *ize* to a noun effectively creates a verb that means doing something that reflects the spirit or attributes of the noun.

Example: "I'm not comfortable with the overly friendly nature of this movie. Where's the conflict? Who are the antagonists? If we're going to sell this idea, I think we need to villainize this script a bit."

What Does It Do?

Weak: "This new centrifugal pump is different because it can move wood chips through pipes."

Powerful: "This is my new *chip thruster.*"

If you create a new device ("Build a better mousetrap?" Oh yeah, we're suppose to avoid that phrase.), you might also be able to create a word based on what it does. My favorite new word for a relatively recent invention? That's easy—the EnvelOpener®, from iSlice.com. It's a covered, ceramic blade that safely and easily opens envelopes. (Incidentally, "EnvelOpener" is also a portmanteau word.) Nifty gadget, nifty name. No wonder that EnvelOpener® is a registered name with the U.S. Patent and Trademark Office.

This type of word trickery doesn't have to be limited to gizmos. You might create a word that explains what a new process does. For example, suppose that you come up with a new way to report errors at work that take lots of hours to correct. Your new method of reporting these boo-boos might be called the Redo Register. Be inventive.

Example: "This new software program takes the employee attributes we're looking for and automatically matches them against key abilities and responses that come out during our screening and interviewing process. I call the program 'Candidate Appraisalator.'"

What Noise Does It Make?

Weak: "It started with an odd click and roar."

Powerful: "It started with an odd ticki-ticki-bam."

This process is more than simply imitating a sound, and it might be a step or two further than creating an *onomatopoeia*.

Instead, the noise might serve as the starting point for a word that describes the mood the noise generates or the feeling you get when you hear that particular noise.

def•i•ni•tion

> **Onomatopoeia** is the formation of a word that sounds like what it is naming. For example, when you say the word *buzz*, it *sounds* like a *buzzz*. *Click* sounds like a click. Other examples abound: *meow, whoosh, ratchet, sizzle,* and so on.

For example, whenever you hear the beginning beats of salsa music, they might make you recall the first time you looked across the room, became enchanted by someone, asked that person to dance, and fell in love. When describing as much in a sentence, you might write, "The boom-badda-badda-badda was overwhelming—was it the music or my heart?"

Example: "The whack-whacketta-whacketta of the machinery is mind-numbing and jarring at once. The use of protective hearing devices is vital for two reasons: the devices protect the workers' hearing and they help workers stay alert so they perform their job tasks accurately and efficiently."

Use a Word from Another Language

Weak: "I love the happiness she brings into a room."

Powerful: "I love the *félicité* she brings into a room."

As the world becomes smaller through communication, travel, and commerce, I suspect we're approaching a time when most people on Earth will speak the same language. I wouldn't be surprised if my children live to see one world language. Which language will it be? Hmmm, that's a tough one. There are reasonable cases for Chinese or English. I suspect that, just as cultures come together and merge, we'll find much the same thing with language.

This phenomenon—this blending—is happening already. We borrow trendy words from other languages, and hip-sounding English words make their way around the world all the time. So, what's the point? You may either fight the tide or swim with it. I suggest that, when an English word just won't do, look into your knowledge of other languages to discover the perfect word. One of my favorites: *la dolce vita*, Italian for "the sweet life." "A rock star's existence of wine, women, and song is truly *la dolce vita*."

You might initially use the word with a brief introduction, or you might use it in such a way that the definition of the word becomes obvious. For example, "Quit being such a *pochemuchka* and mind your own darned business!"

Example: "His miserable *Weltanschauung* brightened instantly at the sight of his first grandchild."

Tie Different Intensities Together

Weak: "The singer sang to a crescendo."

Powerful: "The singer blew us away with her loud-louder-loudest."

It's possible to create a word by tying together different intensities of any particular word. For example, you might write, "I was unimpressed with the brash-and-brasher of his bravado."

It's also possible to tie together opposites with the same impact. "His up-down mood changes were unnerving."

Example: "I love the cute-cuter-cutest smiles of those babies."

Flip Letters

Weak: "She was blissfully ignorant."

Powerful: "She was *issfully blignorant*."

When I say "flip letters," I'm not talking about Vanna White. What I'm talking about is taking two words and playfully switching the beginning of one word with the beginning of the other. Kind of like the drunk who says to the cop, "No, *ossifer*, I haven't *dreen binking!*"

This device might best be used to describe a situation in which confusion prevails. "I'm a bit *waffled* and *webildered* right now." You might want to italicize the flipped words so that the reader understands that you're not simply ignoring the spell-checker on your computer.

Highlight and Delete

Don't use the flipped-letter device in speeches, unless you're relating an anecdote, perhaps. Your audience will think you're either nervous or tipsy.

Believe it or not, the switching of word beginnings has a term. It's called *spoonerism*, a fact that my good friend and wordsmith extraordinaire John Greene recently brought to my attention. Though a spoonerism is generally an accidental occurrence, one could craft a spoonerism for effect. For example, if college students moved into a residence without furniture, they might use a spoonerism to write about it: "It was a *stark, dormy* night."

It's also worth noting that a spoonerism can be used to soften the impact of a profane phrase. But that's not for you, right?

Example: "He tried to *brazzle* us with his *dilliance*."

Once More for the Metaphor

Weak: "She was like a tiger in that room."

Powerful: "She was a tiger in that room."

It seems fitting that this text ends the same way it began—with one more plug for the sturdy, dependable metaphor. It's one thing to say someone acts like a tiger. It's quite another to call him a tiger.

To review: a metaphor is a similarity suggested without using the words *like* or *as*. (When you use *like* or *as*, you're creating a simile.) Instead of comparing by saying how two objects are alike (again, a simile), a metaphor indicates that one object *is* another object.

Instead of writing, "This new day is like a peach, waiting to have a bite taken out of it," write, "I look forward to zestfully biting into this peach that is the new day." Instead of writing, "The future is like a bright horizon," write, "I watch the vivid horizon, full of promise and bright expectations." There's a difference, right?

You can make the association more elusive and unconscious by not referring to one of the two things you're comparing. The obvious example is, "I smell a rat." The implication is that someone is undermining you and that in all likelihood you know who it is. But rather than mention the culprit, you offer this metaphor and keep people intrigued.

Example: "I grasp the power word. It is a sword—strong, cutting, gleaming. It brings me great influence as it commands the attention and respect of others. Oh, great power word. I brandish you with care and pride."

The Least You Need to Know

- It's possible to create words without seeming whimsical or uneducated. In fact, a well-crafted word might find its way into the language.

- Adding a *y* to the end of a noun makes it an adjective. Adding *ize* to the end of a noun makes it a verb. Adding *iac* to the end of a word labels someone who's preoccupied with the word's subject.

- Combining words or flipping words' beginnings are some other ways to find a word or phrase that's the perfect fit for the point you're trying to get across.

- Using nouns as adjectives can be an inventive way to describe something. For example, using a celebrity's name or a movie title as an adjective might be the best way to describe something.

- Sometimes you can give something a new name based on its function or purpose. Apply such a word to a device or a process.

- Sometimes the perfect word is a word from another language. Either define the word when you introduce it, or use it in a context that makes its meaning understandable.

Glossary

buzzword A trendy word with a convincing tone.

cliché A saying that is so overused that its usage is more embarrassing or annoying than clever.

devil's advocate A person who expresses an opposing opinion to provoke debate or to test the soundness of an idea.

dysphemism An impolite word or expression used in place of a more neutral one.

euphemism A mild or polite replacement for an offensive expression or statement.

groupthink A mind-set of compliance that often takes over a group of people. Conformity leads people to agree rather than to question or challenge ideas.

juxtapose To place side-by-side for comparison.

metaphor A comparison made without using *like* or *as*. Example: *Your love is soothing sweetness.*

mirroring A tactic used in active listening; the listener "mirrors," or repeats, some phrases back to the speaker to provoke more openness and more revelations. Mirroring is part of the counseling technique that famous psychologist Carl Rogers called "the reflection of attitudes."

onomatopoeia   The formation of a word that sounds like what it is naming. Examples: *bang, crack, oink.*

portmanteau word   A word formed by combining parts of two other words, usually merging the two words' meanings as well.

proactive   Addressing a problem or personal issue before it takes hold. The antonym, depending on usage, is either "inactive" or "reactive."

rhetorical question   A statement formulated as a question to which no response is expected or necessary.

simile   A figure of speech using either *like* or *as* that compares two things.

tact   A sense of what to say or how to act in order not to offend others.

thesis sentence   A sentence that states the main point and maps out the evidence that will be used to support it.

verbal cue   A word or group of words that signals a transition to the listener.

visceral   Primitive or animal-like, often requiring little or no thought processing.

Appendix B

Suggested Books on Gaining Influence Through Words

Babcock, Linda, and Sara Laschever. *Women Don't Ask: Negotiation and the Gender Divide.* Princeton, NJ: Princeton University Press, 2003.
Economist Linda Babcock and business researcher Sara Laschever argue that one in five adult women today never negotiate over anything. Whether one attributes this notion to the genders being wired differently or to social factors (or both), it's a sad statement that many women don't get what they deserve in life simply because they don't ask. This text, as well as Babcock and Laschever's more recent book *Ask for It* (New York: Bantam, 2009), suggests ways for women to ask and to negotiate.

Callen, Barry. *Perfect Phrases for Sales and Marketing Copy.* New York: McGraw-Hill, 2008.
A must-read for anyone looking to add interest and urgency to his or her writing. Although primarily offered as a text for spicing up commercial copy, this book holds practical advice for any writing situation in which the objective is to catch a reader's

interest or to draw out a reader's positive emotions. Callen takes attention-getting to the next level with great ideas on combining sounds, unique words, or ideas that don't seem to mix until one hears them. Wonderful, experienced thoughts on catchphrases. A quick, pleasant read and reference packed with suggestions.

Carnegie, Dale. *How to Win Friends & Influence People (Reissue Edition)*. New York: Pocket Books, 1990.
Originally written more than 75 years ago, this text remains perhaps the best book ever on getting people to respect you, support you, and do what you ask them to do, often simply by using the right words. If you have a CD player in your car, I recommend the uncondensed audio book version, read by Andrew MacMillan (New York: Simon & Schuster Audio, 1999).

Fox, Jeffrey J. *How to Land Your Dream Job: No Resume and Other Secrets to Get You in the Door*. New York: Hyperion, 2007.
This book was initially released in 2001 under the title *Don't Send a Resume*. It talks about using words to sell yourself as a successful "product." It's a quick but powerful read on how you should present yourself to your bosses (prospective and current) and to your colleagues.

Greene, Robert. *The 48 Laws of Power*. New York: Penguin, 2000.
I don't subscribe to Greene's notion that deceit is a big part of gaining control. In fact, I argue that integrity and authority can go hand-in-hand. However, Greene's advice on choosing the nature and timing of one's words in garnering power is certainly worth the read. The abridged audio book version (Minneapolis, MN: HighBridge Audio, 2007) makes for entertaining commuting. It's read by the masterful Don Leslie.

Heyman, Richard. *How to Say It to Teens: Talking About the Most Important Topics of Their Lives*. Paramus, NJ: Prentice Hall Press, 2001.
This book really should be titled *How to Talk to Anyone Who Won't Listen*. Most of the techniques, words, and phrases offered by Heyman in this text may be used just as effectively in broaching any tough topic with a close acquaintance, regardless of age.

O'Shea, Samara. *For the Love of Letters: A 21st-Century Guide to the Art of Letter Writing.* New York: HarperCollins, 2007.
Rather than examine letter writing as a dying art in an electronic world, this text embraces good letter writing as a necessary part of Internet and instantaneous communication and offers nifty ways to improve both your online and letter-paper prose. (Caution: the book includes a very racy chapter on erotic letter writing.) As a testament to the cool advice in her book, Samara O'Shea's website is www.letterlover.net. She also offers advice via YouTube videos.

Rice, Scott. *Right Words, Right Places.* Belmont, CA: Wadsworth, 1993.
This text is out of print but is very easy to purchase through online used book sellers. Scott Rice is an English professor best known for his "world's worst writer" contest, which he hosts each year at San Jose State University. This particular text does a very nice job blending rules of grammar and rhetoric with effective uses of phrases and opening sentences.

Snair, Scott. *The Complete Idiot's Guide to Motivational Leadership: Surefire Strategies for Encouraging Cooperation.* New York: Alpha Books, 2007.
A good leader needs more than just words for fostering team cohesion and loyalty, but words are a good place to start. This text discusses ways of offering encouragement and praise, methods for offering your team an inspiring vision, and techniques for addressing your team members in a professional, influential manner. I wrote it … I hope you like it.

Tracy, Brian. *Speak to Win: How to Present with Power in Any Situation.* New York: AMACOM, 2008.
Brian Tracy is the quintessential expert on "closing the deal" with the right words. This text discusses how to offer great presentations to both large and small groups. Also recommended: any of Tracy's audio books on leadership and success, for an informative ride in the car.

The Power Word Checklist

Before you write your next letter, give your next speech, or attend your next important meeting, check one or more of the following lists. They might remind you about a hint or two that you read earlier in this guide.

Power Writing

❏ You understand that the first rule in power writing is to keep the reader reading.

❏ You suggest from the start that what you're communicating is imperative and undeniable. You portray the situation or the argument as monumental.

❏ You suggest that time and resources are running out and that the reader better act quickly.

❏ Your writing is authoritative but not condescending.

❏ You state up front what you would like accomplished or resolved. You are polite but persistent.

❏ You pack your writing with emotion, appealing to the reader's optimism and empathy.

❏ You write in a way that assumes the reader's agreement and consent.

❏ When appropriate, you write with dramatic extremes and contrasts.

❏ You begin with a hypothetical situation or a magnificent vision of what the future could be like.

❏ You portray yourself in your writing as being on your reader's side.

❏ You design your first sentence or two to hook your reader and keep him or her interested.

❏ You suggest to your readers that they are in the middle of an important part of history and that they have become important players in that history.

❏ You use artistic metaphors by making comparisons without using the words *like* or *as*.

❏ You state the problem, its causes, and your proposed solution right away in your argument.

❏ Your arguments, while well supported, often go against the grain.

❏ You often write grateful, handwritten letters on nice stationery and you mail them through the U.S. Postal Service, sometimes even to people in your own office.

❏ You use the word *I* to punctuate how something is affecting you or to assume personal ownership of your argument and its solution.

❏ You rightfully take credit for your ideas, but you offer them in your writing from a standpoint of humility.

❏ You begin all your written requests with a sincere compliment and an appeal to the reader's generosity.

❏ At the end of your written proposal, you emphasize how your suggestion will bring about something the reader currently needs or lacks.

❑ You wrap up your recommendation by accentuating its positive points.

❑ You appeal to people's overriding desire to save time, money, and aggravation.

❑ You sprinkle your argumentative writing with expert endorsements, added value, appeals to security, and repeated keywords.

❑ You avoid clichéd words or phrases.

❑ You appeal to people's egos, sense of worth, and humanistic sense of responsibility.

Power Speaking

❑ When you speak, you appeal to people's love for their patriarch or matriarch.

❑ You appeal to people's love for and dedication to their team or their cause.

❑ You are very specific about what you promise.

❑ You are very detailed about what you see wrong and how you'd like things fixed.

❑ You speak in the active voice, avoiding phrases such as, "It has been decided that ..." You don't hide behind your suggestions or decisions.

❑ With your words, you try to make people feel good about their successes and about themselves.

❑ You say things that prompt people to think good things about you and about themselves. You say nice, positive things that make people remember you.

❑ You always remind people that you respect their skills, that you trust them with tasks, and that you count on them to make big things happen.

❑ You utter phrases that make people feel valued and wanted.

❏ You say affirmative things that make people feel good about belonging to a team, a family, or an organization.

❏ You regularly offer compliments and words of gratitude. Whenever you can, you follow up with handwritten thank-you notes.

Power Replying

❏ You always respond in a positive way, even if there's little cause for positive thinking.

❏ Often, you prefer to listen and nod as opposed to replying.

❏ You apply effective, proven listening skills.

❏ You address issues or circumstances that can be changed.

❏ Instead of offering excuses, you own your mistake and say "no excuse."

❏ You explain to someone exactly what is upsetting you.

❏ You refer to what the average person might say were he or she to hear the same thing.

❏ You offer a smooth, confident, relaxed air that puts people at ease.

❏ You don't mind conceding the point (or losing a battle) if it means gaining the ultimate goal (or winning the war).

❏ If you're putting up a defensive front, it's not apparent to others.

❏ You thank someone for correcting one of your facts rather than getting defensive.

❏ You don't demean other people's ideas, no matter how silly those ideas might seem initially.

❏ When someone asks how you're doing, you reply with something spectacular, other than simply saying, "Fine."

Power Evading

❏ You avoid hiding behind sentences in the passive voice—you own your thoughts, challenges, decisions, and success stories.

❏ You don't ever tell people that they're flat-out wrong, even if they are. Doing so would only put up a wall of resistance.

❏ You avoid forcing people to change. Instead, you appeal to their general sense of decency, charity, and respect for the big picture.

❏ You avoid ostracizing people. Instead, you appeal to their general desire to belong to a group or be a part of something bigger than themselves.

❏ You avoid long lists of supporting points. Instead, you keep your main argumentative points limited to three at a time.

❏ You avoid laundry lists of demands. Instead, you keep your list of requests limited to two or three practical appeals at one time.

Power Gaming

❏ You appreciate that the ultimate goal in your power-word gaming is to get your way and not to win the argument.

❏ You allow the other person the dignity of not having to admit outright that he or she is wrong. That is, you concede that you *might* be wrong while still asking for something to be corrected.

❏ You know what a rhetorical question is. You plant in your conversation rhetorical questions about the person's overriding (and underlying) concerns and beliefs.

❏ Your proposals explain the solution by combining just a few simple words. ("This is a pay-for-performance salary plan.")

❏ You appeal to most people's innate desire to follow instructions and authority.

❏ You begin requests with a corny compliment. It won't come across as all that corny.

❏ You assume consent until you're told otherwise (except on a date).

❏ You never stop telling people how much you appreciate them.

Index

Q

R

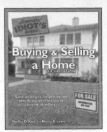